ANATOLY NAZIROV

АНАТОЛИЙ НАЗИРОВ

A Poet's Gallery
Галерея

Translated from the Russian by
Ivan Zhavoronkov
Edited by John Woodsworth

Перевёл на английский язык
Иван Жаворонков
Редактор Джон Вудсворт

Toronto 2011
Торонто

A Poet's Gallery. Галерея. *Toronto 2011.*
Translated from the Russian by Ivan Zhavoronkov,
Edited by John Woodsworth.
Copyright Translation © 2005 by Ivan Zhavoronkov.
Drawings: Parthenos *by Elena Makarova;*
Sun and Eagle *by R. I. Suslova*
(reprinted from "Заратустра")
All rights reserved. No part of this book may be used
or reproduced in any manner whatsoever
without written permission.

Permission obtained to publish English translation
by John Woodsworth. Russian poems reprinted
from "Галерея" (Санкт-Петербург – 2001) and
"Заратустра" (по мотивам произведения Ф. Ницше
"Так говорил Заратустра". Философская поэма.
Санкт-Петербург – 1993) by Anatoly Nazirov
upon consent of the author.

For more information on edition or to place an order,
please email at: zarathustra2001us@yahoo.com

ISBN: 0-9737762-0-X

A Poet's Gallery. 161 pages
Page format: 6" x 9"
Cover Design by Ivan Zhavoronkov
2011•Published by York University

Published by York University in Toronto.
Printed in Canada.

A Poet's Gallery

Галерея

A Poet's Gallery. Anatoly Nazirov

Галерея. Анатолий Назиров

CONTENTS

Editor's Foreword..11
Translation as Domestication of the Self:
Anatoly Nazirov's *Zarathustra*..17

Стихи. Poems:

Лес поэзии...46
In the Wood of Poetry..47

Гудок...48
The Ship's Blast...49

Юность..48
Youth...49

О себе..50
About Myself...51

«Букету полевых цветов...»...50
"My Heartache..."...51

«Моим мечтам даримая...»...50
"You Have Been Passing By..."...51

«Ты в детстве в куклы не играла...»...............................52
"You, as a Little Girl..."...53

«Я вдохнулся в слова...»..52
"I Breathed Upon My Words...".......................................53

«Обо мне вспоминаешь редко...»..................................52
"You Remember Me..."...53

«Во время таянья снегов...»..54
"When Winter's Snows..."...55

«Без тебя мне май...»..54
"Spring Without You..."..55

«Для чего мне цветы на поляне...»......................54
"Why Care I For Flowers..."......................................55

«То луной лукавой...»..56
"First You, Sly As..."..57

Проволока..56
Barbed Wire..57

«Блаженства суть яви, открой...»........................58
"Reveal the Sense of Bliss..."....................................59

«Тебе меня немного не хватает...»......................58
"You Miss Me..."..59

«Сказала ты...»...60
"You've told me..."..61

«Ты вошла в меня...»..60
"You this Life of Mine..."..61

«Во мгле прибой...»..60
"The Surging Surf..."..61

Размолвка..62
Disengagement..63

Примирение..64
Reconciliation..65

Согласие..64
Harmony..65

Женщине..66
To a Woman...67

«Ты наговором серебрила...»..................................66
"You Spoke a Silver Spell..."...................................67

«Твои глаза отчаянно молчали...».........................68
"Your Eyes..."..69

Весна...68
Spring..69

Пейзаж..70
Landscape..71

Эскиз...70
Sketch..71

Сон...72
Dreaming...73

Рыжая дама (перевод на англ. Джона Вудсворта).....72
The Red-Haired Lady (translated by John Woodsworth).....73

Натюрморт..74
Still Life..75

Дочери...74
To My Daughter...75

«Отчего ушёл?» спросила...».....................................76
" 'Why'd he go?'..."..77

«Какая горькая истома...»...76
Bitter Languish..77

«Когда безмятежные йоги...».....................................78
"When Yogis Walk Barefoot..."...................................79

«Очисти дух, и взоры оживут...»...............................78
"Cleanse the Spirit..."..79

«Я признаюсь, я – не охотник...»......................................80
"Admittedly, I'm not a Hunter...".....................................81

Антоний и Клеопатра..80
Antony and Cleopatra...81

Гойя герцогине Альба...82
Goya to the Dutchess of Alba...83

Портрет Индиры Ганди...82
Portrait of Indira Gandhi..83

«Да, жизнь – растерянный калека...».....................................82
"Yes, Life is..."...83

Влюблённый фонарь...84
The Love-Sick Street-Lamp...85

«Сердце шаманит ударами бубна...».......................................84
"Heart-pounding Shaman's Drum...".......................................85

Есенинский мотив..84
Inspired by Esenin..85

Красноуральск...86
Krasnouralsk..87

Назарет...86
Nazareth..87

Горе..88
Sorrow..89

Суд...88
Judgement...89

Раздумье..90
Meditation 91

«О понимании творения в стихах...» (*Памяти Л.Н. Мартынова*)
(Перевод Ивана Жаворонкова
и Джона Вудсворта)..90
"The Sounds of the Lines..."[*In Memory of L.N.Martynov*]
(Co-translation by Ivan Zhavoronkov
and John Woodsworth)..91

Рождение философии из духа поэзии
(Перевод Ивана Жаворонкова
и Джона Вудсворта)..92
The Birth of Philosophy from the Spirit of Poetry
(Co-translation by Ivan Zhavoronkov
and John Woodsworth)..93

Пульс мира..96
The Pulse of the World..97

ЗАРАТУСТРА
  (*Посвящается памяти поэта
  Леонида Николаевича Мартынова*):
ZARATHUSTRA
  [*Dedicated to the memory of the poet
  Leonid Nikolayevich Martynov*]:

  Заратустра в долине..106
  Zarathustra In the Valley..107

  Речи Заратустры..122
  Zarathustra's Speeches..123

  Заратустра в городе..132
  Zarathustra In Town..133

  Возвращение Заратустры..140
  Zarathustra's Return..141

  Тихий час..158
  The Quiet Hour..159

Editor's Foreword

When Russian native speaker Ivan Zhavoronkov first approached me in March 2005 about editing his translations of poetry from Russian into English, I must admit I had some misgivings about taking on the task. As a professional Russian-English translator, I have generally found it true that revising a non-native speaker's English translation of a prose text involves considerably more work than making my own translation from scratch, and I tend to avoid it.

However, as someone with a particular interest in poetic translation, I was intrigued by the challenge Zhavoronkov had set himself in his efforts to translate *poetry* from his native Russian into English. We had something in common, he and I (in addition to our first names: Russian *Ivan* and English *John* are both derived from Greek *Ioannes*): I myself have attempted on occasion to translate poetry from my native English into Russian, as well as to write my own poems in Russian — with varying degrees of success (though a number of print media and Internet websites have seen fit to publish them). After due consideration, I decided to accept Mr Zhavoronkov's invitation to edit his work — partly on a professional basis, partly as a 'labour of love'.

When I started, I had little idea of how long the resulting book would be (had I known its extent in advance, I might not have started at all!), but now that *A poet's gallery* is finally ready for publication, I can honestly say I have no regrets.

I was also impressed by the thoughtful analysis of the whole task of translation as 'domestication', as outlined in Ivan Zhavoronkov's accompanying essay, which I had not had the opportunity to read until very recently. So much of what he says there strikes a familiar chord with my own forty-five-year experience as a translator, in particular the need to achieve what he aptly calls *the golden mean.* This refers to the optimum balance between preserving both the cultural and linguistic flavour of the source-language while at the same time making the translation sound 'at home' in the target language — i.e., not *too* foreign, yet not so far removed from the original that it becomes an artistic transposition rather than a translation. One could (to offer an extreme hypothetical example) transpose a story about Russia under Catherine the Great to nineteenth-century Britain under Queen Victoria, but while that might be easier for anglophone readers to relate to, it could hardly be called a 'translation'. Yet the translation should sound sufficiently natural as to enable the reader to follow the story (or poem) in a smooth flow, without stopping at every sentence (or stanza) to poke holes through the barrier of 'foreignness'. In other words, it should sound 'domesticated'.

A good poetry translator always tries to convey in the target language the 'suprasegmental' features of the original (especially *rhyme* and *metre,* where applicable). It is interesting to note that in much of his poetry, including almost all of *Zarathustra,* Anatoly Nazirov has departed from the strict classical rhyme-schemes still observed in most Russian poetry today. Indeed, this actually brings him closer to the 'unrhymed' model characteristic of most modern poetry in English, though throughout his poems he still holds on (more or less) to a pre-determined *metre* (akin to blank verse). While the translator has put every effort into preserving Nazirov's original Russian metre — not an easy task, mind you — certain liberties in conveying the rhythm could not be avoided, especially in the observance of so-called 'masculine' (stress on final syllable) versus 'feminine' (penultimate syllable stressed) line-endings.

The poet does feature *rhyme* in a number of his poems, and here again Ivan Zhavoronkov has made a consistent and conscientious attempt to reproduce the rhyme-scheme whenever one is apparent in the original. As a long-time poetic translator myself, I can attest that English is at a particular disadvantage compared to Russian when it comes to rhyme in poetry, as quite a few Russian grammatical endings (especially in the present tense of verbs, but also with certain cases of nouns and adjectives) are common to a vast number of words (cf. the ending *-ation* in English), making it very easy to find a rhyme for just about any verb and quite a few nouns and adjectives. English grammar, unfortunately, does not possess similar uniform properties — in fact, English has very few grammatical endings to begin with, other than *-(e)s, -(e)d* and *-ing,* which are hardly useful for rhyming purposes. This 'deficiency' makes the challenge of finding corresponding rhymes in the translation all the more difficult.

Even so, here, too, the translator has acquitted himself well. One striking example is his rendition of the six-line poem "Горе" [pronounced: *GOR-ya*], meaning "Sorrow", in which a single rhyme (or assonance) pervades the whole piece. Below you may compare the translation with the original Russian, with approximate pronunciation shown in a rough English transcription (stressed syllables in caps):

GOR-ya [Russian original]   Sorrow [*Zhavoronkov's translation*]

sa-GLAS-na GAY-gal-yu, u GOR-ya   As Hegel holds, inside of sorrow
vnu-TREE sve-CHEN-i-ya dru-GO-ya: There is a different light to borrow:
kak mal-cha-LEE-vast pri u-KOR-ya.   Keep silent when reproached tomorrow.
kak re-ya-GEAR-a-vat na GOR-ya?   How should you treat befalling sorrow?
kak na pred-GOR-ya,   Just like the hollow
kag-DA pad-NIAT-sa NA-dav GO-ru.   As up the mount you have to follow.

Here the translator manages to convey the uniform rhyme/assonance of the original through all six lines of the poem, as well as the original metre, and does so with minimal departure from the literal meaning (e.g., while *pred-GOR-ya* literally means 'foothill', the associated word 'hollow' — i.e., what lies between foothills — conveys the meaning adequately enough).

Note that *assonance* (or partial rhyme — e.g., *sorrow/hollow*) is a standard component of the poetic translator's tool-kit, expanding rhyming possibilities even in cases where the original poet confines himself to strict rhyme. Nazirov himself, however, frequently employs assonance (e.g., *GOR-ya/GO-ya/GO-ru*) as well as exact rhyme (*GOR-ya/u-KOR-ya*), so in such poems assonance is quite at home in the translation, too. In another of Nazirov's poems, entitled "Эскиз" [pron. *es-KEES*], or "Sketch", where every word in the original poem has a rhyming counterpart, Zhavoronkov has ingeniously managed to capture that feature in the translation. In an e-mail to me he noted that "...the poet himself had strong misgivings concerning a translation of this poem before I finally translated it. He said categorically that it was untranslatable... However, these words of his induced me to work even harder and come up with English equivalents to convey the rhymes/assonances of the original and still preserve the overall meaning of the poem."

A noteworthy discrepancy between Russian and English poetry is that English words, destitute as they are of grammatical endings, are generally shorter than Russian words, which means fewer syllables are required to express equivalent meanings. Thus the Russian-English translator is constantly obliged to add words (or, more precisely, syllables) to make up the number of feet required by the original metre. The general rule is to add words which in themselves have either (a) little semantic content or (b) a semantic content that is *implied in* (or at least *in keeping with*) the original poem. Such additions in the example quoted above are: (a) *inside of* and (b) *borrow, tomorrow* and *befalling,* without which the poem's overall iambic tetrameter (the dimeter of the penultimate line being an exception) would be shy of the requisite number of syllables. But there is a silver lining here: the translator can often use such an addition to achieve a required rhyme (as in *borrow* and *tomorrow* for *sorrow*).

Further, Nazirov's original poems feature many instances of *word-play* (note *GOR-ya* [sorrow] set against both *pred-GOR-ya* [foothill] and *GO-ru* [mountain] in the above example). Such word-play is perhaps the trickiest element to convey in any translation, since it involves (often random) co-incidences of meaning specific to the source-language which almost never have a direct equivalent in the target language, and so the poetic translator's ingenuity is really put to the test. Sometimes this involves finding target-language word-play possibilities elsewhere in the poem to compensate. This extends to the concept of what one might call *implicit compensation* (where the reader is left to connect the dots and deduce the hidden word-play). The translator described such a phenomenon in a recent e-mail — in reference to his translation of this particular poem:

> ...although there is no equivalent for this significant word-play Горе/Гора (Cf. Sorrow/Mountain) in the English language, on which the whole idea of the poem is based, target-language word-play possibilities may be implicitly traced through "mount" as a noun (mountain) to "mount" as a verb (to mount). As a result, "As up the mount you have to follow" invokes the picture of one *mounting* the *mount*(ain) and thus sur*mount*ing it. In addition, (the a*mount* of) Sorrow, that has to be overcome or sur*mount*ed, is on the one hand compared with (what a*mounts*

to) a Mount(ain) in greatness and on the other reduced to a Hollow (both on the level of contextual meaning and assonance) as one *mount*s, or sur*mount*s, the *mount*(ain). The word-play is implicit in the target language (in my translation), it only has to be discovered…

I shall not comment further here, as Zhavoronkov has already dealt with the device of compensation most interestingly in his introductory essay (note especially his remark on "the 'lie' of the serpent").

Another challenging phenomenon for the translator of Nazirov's poetry in particular is *word-coinage,* which is also described at length in his essay.

Suffice it to say that Ivan Zhavoronkov's status as a native speaker of Russian endows him with a particular sensitivity to the nuances of Russian poetics, including rhyme, metre and word-play, and so his constant attention to the need to preserve them in the translation — insofar as the norms of poetic English will allow — forms an integral component of the 'domestication' process.

I do agree with Zhavoronkov's claim that there is much to be said for a 'domesticated' translation by one more familiar (through life-experience) with the source language (in this case, Russian) than the target language (English), even if such a translation requires editing before being set forth for direct consumption by an anglophone reading public. And I hope you will agree with me that this claim is justified — and to a significant degree — in the work of Anatoly Nazirov's poetry now before you, as translated and 'domesticated' (with a little help from yours truly) by Ivan Zhavoronkov.
Happy reading!

Ottawa (Canada) John Woodsworth
4 January 2011 Member, Literary Translators'
  Association of Canada
  http://kanadacha.ca

John Woodsworth, B.A. (UBC), M.A. (Simon Fraser Univ.), has been a translator (mainly Russian-English) for 45 years and is currently Administrative Assistant and Research Associate with the Slavic Research Group at the University of Ottawa. A member of the Literary Translators' Association of Canada, he has published 23 book translations, including the popular 9-volume *Ringing Cedars Series* by Vladimir Megré and, most recently, *My life* — the autobiography of Sofia Andreevna Tolstaya (Leo Tolstoy's wife), co-translated with Arkadi Klioutchanski under the editorship of renowned Tolstoy expert Andrew Donskov. He specialises in poetry translation, having 178 published poem translations to his credit, along with 98 publications of his original poetry in Russian. See his website at: http://kanadacha.ca

Translation as Domestication of the Self:
Anatoly Nazirov's *Zarathustra*
by Ivan Zhavoronkov

Introduction

This research is devoted to the study of my own translation of Anatoly Nazirov's *Zarathustra,* inspired by Friedrich Nietzsche's *Thus Spake Zarathustra.* Anatoly Nazirov's poem is in and of itself a brilliant attempt to re-interpret, one hundred years later, Nietzsche's masterpiece.

Nazirov's *Zarathustra* is a highly philosophical and lyrical work, challenging to translate from the great Russian language into the no less great English language. Things get even more complicated when the role of translator falls to me, as English is not a native language for me, not one acquired or spoken since infancy. The problem of translation, as I see it, consists in the limitations of the translator's English-language competence as contrasted with that of the native-English-speaking editor of the translation, who himself is a Russian-to-English translator and poet living and working in Ottawa, Canada.

In my research, I wanted to determine what it meant for me to translate Nazirov's *Zarathustra* from my native language, Russian, into my second language, English. The claim of this paper is that my translation of the poem is rather a *domestication* of the original. By the latter I am referring to the translation learning curve from my native Russian to my foreign English (as opposed to Lawrence Venuti's consideration of *domestication* from the standpoint of the native-English-speaking translator-theorist). In other words, I have endeavoured to make a translation that will be quite readable in English without excessive russification of the English language, and the more English-sounding a translation I can make, the more successful I shall be as a non-native-speaking translator. Translation as *conquest*, a principle I have adopted from Nietzsche, underlies my translation goal (and will be defined).

In converse parallel with Victor Hugo, I lay emphasis on my learning contribution to my foreign rather than my native language, which will give an afterlife (in the Walter Benjamin sense) to the original and disprove Schleiermacher's statement that good translation from native to foreign language is a wicked art, and — following Goethe — attempt to strike a balance between the foreign and domestic as a prerequisite for a continuing domestication that must be guided (as Herder suggests about the ideal translator) by the principle of philosophy, philology and poetry combined.

Further, the major differences between Russian and English are outlined with a view to promoting a general understanding of the incommensurability of these two languages, especially in grammar and semantics. According to Leonardo Bruni, one must have a good knowledge of both source and target languages.

A practical analysis of my translation of Nazirov's *Zarathustra* will explore the incommensurability of the original text with the target language while drawing upon particular examples from the poem; this will be followed by my own translation with comments by my editor, establishing the validity of the preference of domestication over foreignisation of the translation as a learning-contribution curve on my part as a Russian-to-English translator. Word-coinages, alliteration and assonance, diminutive words and the syntactical semantic incommensurability of Russian and English languages will constitute the corpus of the practical analysis, as these are central to the philosophical poem — unique in tone and informed by the personal life-experiences of the poet.

The general conclusion will be made at the end of the paper that translating poetry from native to foreign language, as in my case, is worth the attempt, that it is a legitimate way of learning and understanding a foreign language and culture, and, most importantly, that translation as domestication is the lighthouse by which the translator orients himself in the twilight of translation in the hope of setting foot on the foreign shore of the Other, and that it is also finding oneself at home in the foreignness of the Other.

The selected bibliography serves as the basis for my research, which will also make use of Nietzsche's main philosophical ideas as expanded upon by Martin Heidegger, showing that challenging tasks such as mine must be taken on by translators who are at the same time philosophers, philologists, and poets — the qualities of the Nietzschean Overman.

In his preface to his translations of Shakespeare, Victor Hugo said of poetry translation: "To translate a foreign writer is to add to your own national poetry" (Lefevere 18). My case is the reverse of what Hugo described. I intend to contribute to the English language and at the same time learn the target language of my contribution. Thus, translation in my case, where a poem written in my native language, Russian, finds its expression in my second language, English, is a learning contribution and (as such) reciprocal. While I am adding to the English language and culture, they themselves are adding to my knowledge of them. The learning cycle is endless, as is the contribution. Therefore, my translation can never be said to be completed.

My translation does not aim at the foreignness of the original in light of the target language; rather, it seeks ways for the original to depart from and direct itself toward and end up in the target language as its new home. In "The Task of the Translator", Walter Benjamin writes that "no translation would be possible if in its ultimate essence it strove for likeness to the original" (73). In my translation of Nazirov's *Zarathustra* from the Russian into English, I strive to give an afterlife (as Walter Benjamin calls it) to the original poem so that my translation may become an "echo of the original" (76) to be heard and responded to in the context of the English language and culture.

Even though anglophones do not possess the original of the poem, they will be able to receive into their *home* a *domesticated* translation. Even with the most domesticated translation, however, the foreignness still sneaks in: the ideas and the way they are put together in the translation as guided by the overall structure of the original, from which the translator cannot deviate (unless it is an independent piece of poetry inspired by the original), are always new — therefore to a certain extent foreign — yet they become acceptable through the domesticating process permeating the whole translation. Translation *is* a domestication, without which the original never comes across.

While I quite agree with Walter Benjamin that literal (word-for-word) translation enriches the target language, I do not wish to see my English translation impoverished by lack of domestication. The target language always gives preference to itself, that is, to domestication. It cannot tolerate much, if any, obvious foreignness. Therefore, it accepts and receives into itself what is acceptable and receivable of the original, whose natural state in the target language is domestication.

According to Lawrence Venuti's "Translation, Community, Utopia", "the domesticating process... operate[s] in every word of the translation..." (468). Domestication alters the meaning of the original: it makes lexico-semantic shifts coupled by use of idiomatic expressions (471). Translation is possible only as partial communication "both incomplete and inevitably slanted towards the domestic scene" (473). Yet a translation closer to the original text conveys more of the spirit of the original. One of the reasons that I have endeavoured to domesticate my translation of *Zarathustra* is that, as Venuti writes, "[t]he domestic inscription in the translation extends the appeal of the foreign text to a mass audience in another culture" (482), but at the same time I try to preserve the foreignness of the original by preserving the overall structure of the poem.

My translation has nothing to do with ideology, and I disagree with Venuti when he says: "Translating is always ideological because it releases a domestic remainder, an inscription of values, beliefs, and representations linked to historical moments and social positions in the domestic culture" (485). My goal is to domesticate my translation in order to make it more readable in terms of the standards of the English language. Besides that, the philosophical content of the poem always stands above culture and, hopefully, above all ideology.

The poem *Zarathustra*, as well as my translation, aims at wisdom, thinking and seeking truth above the human — above what is inculcated by beliefs, customs, traditions and all kinds of ideologies. This is philosophy and poetry blended together, that is, thinking profoundly in beautiful images. Again, Venuti writes:

> Translating releases a surplus of meanings which refer to domestic cultural traditions through deviations from the current standard dialect or otherwise standardized languages — through archaisms, for example, or colloquialisms. Implicit in any translation is the hope for a consensus, a communication and recognition of the foreign text through a domestic inscription. (485)

My 'domestic inscription' in the poem is free from any hidden motives to insinuate any domestic content mixed with the foreign that would somehow sway the mind of the reader politically, ideologically or otherwise. My choice of words favours neutrality along with accuracy of meaning. Still, foreign constituencies, Venuti is certain, must be preserved on the domestic scene (488), and in my view these should necessarily be devoid of ideological intentions. Rather, my translation strives to convey the emotional world of the character Zarathustra as informed by the poet's personal experiences. My translation is a meticulous searching for words that would render the diversity of human character from Russian into English.

I would equate foreignisation of the translation of *Zarathustra* with literal rendition, what Friedrich Schleiermacher calls — in "On the Three Different Methods of Translating" — "a merely mechanical task that can be performed by anyone with a modest proficiency in both languages..." (Robinson 227). Translation as imitation — according to Schleiermacher, producing the same effect on the target language reader as the original does on the source language reader (Robinson 229) — is what I associate with the same perception of the text in both languages as *adequacy,* which means domestication. Through domestication I am at home in the Russian. My Russian sense of being at home aims to feel just as well at home in the English translation.

Moreover, it is not just a question of siding with the author of *Zarathustra.* I actually consider this poem as my own, written by me, and from my own heart in this Russian poem I proceed with the translation of it from *my* Russian into what is *not yet* my English. I want to represent my native tongue in the foreign language. My 'nativeness' has the advantage of being native over the native being foreign to the foreign.

My translating *Zarathustra* from the Russian into English is in a way an attempt to refute the commonly held opinion that translation should only proceed from a foreign into one's native language. Schleiermacher is very certain that if one attempts "to write just as well and as originally in the foreign language", he "would unhesitatingly pronounce it a wicked and magical art akin to going doubled, an attempt at once to flout the laws of nature and to perplex others", and that "[w]riting in a foreign language is never original" (Robinson 236). This "magical art" must first be allowed, before it produces majestic art.

In his treatise "Poetry and Truth", Johann Wolfgang von Goethe, one of the greatest German romantic writers, favours prose translations of poetry. "I consider prose translations more profitable than poetic ones," he says, adding in reference to Luther's translation of the Bible, that "[a] simple translation always remains best for the masses, who have to feel an effect" (Robinson 222). In "Oration in Memory of Wieland, Our Noble Poet, Brother, and Friend", out of the "two maxims for translation" (Robinson 222) — whether to enter and remain within the world of the original or to bring that world over and adapt it to ours to explore our own world, or even a combination of both as a possible third maxim — Goethe prefers the second. Yet, toward the end of "West-Östlicher Divan", Goethe envisions "the alien and the familiar, the known and the unknown move toward each other" (Robinson 224). This is similar to the privilege (which in itself presupposes a combination) of what I call domestication over foreignisation in translation of Nazirov's *Zarathustra*. This approach possesses traits of wisdom, philosophical introspection and search for truth by constantly redefining it in the light of one's own perspectives on self- and world interpretations through intellectual honesty as one's only virtue (in the Nietzschean sense) as the most spiritual will to power.

In his article "On the More Recent German Literature: Fragments", Johann Gottfried von Herder gives a wonderful definition of an ideal translator by way of a hopeful question: "Where is the translator who is at once a philosopher, philologist, and poet? He shall be the morning star of a new day in our literature" (Robinson 207). This reminds us of Nietzsche's conception of the Overman in Heidegger's interpretation in his *Nietzsche* volumes: the Overman is understood as a synthesis of art (cf. Herder's "poet"), philosophy and science (cf. Herder's "philologist").

In one of my other essays entitled *The Evolution of the Übermensch in Nietzsche's ALSO SPRACH ZARATHUSTRA Through Translation*,[1] I explore how different English translations of the term

---

[1] See "Поэтика Ницше. Межвузовский сборник начных статей." - СПб.: Изд-во СПбГУСЭ, 2010. - 183 с. Стр. 143 – 163. [*Poetika Nietzsche. Mezhvuzovskiy sbornik nauchnykh statey*. St-Petersburg: St-Petersburg State University of Service and Economics, 2010. - 183 pages in total; pp.143 – 163.]

Übermensch elicit different meanings that correspond to all three constituents of the Nietzschean overman as the aforementioned synthesis. Thomas Common (19th–20th centuries) translates *Übermensch* as *superman*, Walter Kaufmann (1950s) as *overman*, and Graham Parkes (21st century) as *overhuman*. My analysis of these translations reveal that 'superman' is a poetical translation, 'overman' a philosophical, and 'overhuman' a philological, hence scientific, translation. The evolution of the *Übermensch* from the poet to the philosopher to the scientist corresponds to Anatoly Nazirov's historical-philosophical analysis of thinking in his "Stages in the Development of Thinking Within Culture" and *The Philosophy of Science,* namely that thinking historically undergoes translations from poetry to philosophy and finally to science.

Interestingly, Herder talks of a kind of translator who would combine all those three qualities, and the resulting individual possessing such characteristics, according to Nietzsche, will be the *Übermensch*. The *Übermensch* is the human being who conquers him- or herself eternally in a spiritual self-overcoming process, creates and recreates values, translates himself from the last man into the overman. Furthermore, Nietzsche himself writes in *The Gay Science* on translation as conquest (136–138): for Romans, "translation was a form of conquest" (137) and should remain as such forever, so as to push boundaries toward the overhuman (as for me, I 'conquer translation' when my translation sounds poetic and at the same time not awkward to native speakers). Similarly, my task is to translate myself from thinking in Russian to thinking in English, from the foreigner I am to being naturalised and domesticated. Nazirov's *Zarathustra* as a lyrical philosophical poem presents itself as a synthesis of philosophy as thinking, philology as science, and poetry as art. Apparently, the translator must possess the respective qualities in order to be challenged by the kind of poem *Zarathustra* is.

2. Native vs. Foreign Language

An anonymous twelfth-century commentator on Boethius' *De Arithmetica* distinguishes three types of translation: first, sense-for-sense, "when only the substance is transmitted"; second, "the substance is transmitted and the sense of the words is preserved"; and third, both the substance and the sense of the words are conveyed in a word-for-word translation (Robinson 43). The third type of translation that the anonymous commentator singles out is an ideal one and, due to the incompatibility of languages in general, is extremely rare, if possible at all. This would depend, first and foremost, on the specificity of language structure and, secondly, on the cultures in which the source and target languages are embedded.

A high degree of kinship between source and target languages and cultures will allow for a word-for-word translation without the loss of the original substance in the target text. The pairing of Russian and Ukrainian, for example, offers a wonderful opportunity for ideal translation. English and Russian, however, are another story as they belong to different language groups: Germanic and Slavic respectively.

The first striking difference between these two languages is the *word order.* English has a strict and accurate structure that must follow the Subject-Predicate-Object order with admissible variational departures from the commonly acceptable linguistic norms, especially in poetry. This limited admissibility would to a certain degree facilitate the translation process of Russian poetry into English. Russian, on the other hand, is much more flexible. It allows easily for practically any kind of word order in ordinary as well as in literary Russian, and especially in poetry. Many more shades of meaning may be expressed through such word-order variations in Russian than in the English.

As far as the language structure alone is concerned, it is just as unique to the Russian language as it is to the poet himself. Pronouns may be freely omitted in Russian, the predicate often precedes the subject, and within the sentence structure the adjective may be far away from the noun it modifies, and that without loss of meaning and the beauty thereof. In fact, such a word order may only enhance the beautiful meaning of the poem, making it more lofty and elevated in style and, again, bringing in the poet's personal attitude towards the versification itself.

In his article "On the Correct Way to Translate", Leonardo Bruni expounds on what correct translation actually involves. He writes that "the whole essence of translation is to transfer correctly what is written in one language into another language", and for that purpose one must necessarily have "a wide and extensive knowledge of both languages."

Further he elaborates on what he means by such knowledge, defining it as "one that is wide, idiomatic, accurate and detailed, acquired from a long reading of the philosophers and orators and poets and all other writers" (Robinson 58). That is, according to Bruni, one should have as much knowledge of both languages and literatures available to him or her in both languages as possible in order to execute an excellent accurate translation of a complex text from one language to another, while preserving the rhythmical qualities, the style, the figures of speech and thought, and thereby the whole majesty of the original text. One must note, however, that Bruni, while taking into consideration all the major principles of translation, is silent on whether the translator should have native (or near-native) command of both languages or only of one language; and if only one, then would it be the source or target language?

My understanding — and it is commonly believed that the translator should always translate into his or her own tongue — is that the translator must be well acquainted, to say the least, with the source language, even if it is not his mother tongue. On the other hand — assuming the translator is a native speaker of the target language, his accuracy of understanding of the latter is surely guaranteed, even though there may be a question of degree. There would seem to be no questioning of the axiom that it is impossible to know a foreign language better than one's own.

The opposite scenario would be when the translator undertakes a translation from his or her native language into a foreign tongue that s/he knows fairly well. The axiom quoted above suggests that, because knowledge of one's mother tongue is always superior to that of a foreign language, the excellency and accuracy of the translation from native to foreign language is always subject to verification and accuracy is not immediately guaranteed. This does not automatically mean, however, that translations from native to foreign languages are not welcome and should not therefore be undertaken as a rule.

In fact, there is one counter-argument that I would like to advance immediately, namely, that the translator who is a native speaker of the source rather than the target language (as in the present case: Nazirov as author and I as his translator) has the advantage of being intimately acquainted with all the subtleties of the source language and culture. If one thinks of it, a language native from birth is perceived by its speakers as a continuous flow and any interruption in the form of a semantic or other deviation from this flow at once causes a rough wave, a ripple, or uneven surface, which is not expected or desired but is all of a sudden stumbled upon in the target text.

One can be said to have but a limited knowledge of *any* language one speaks, especially a foreign one. It would follow, therefore, that my translation from Russian to English would be more deficient than one undertaken in the opposite direction. In either case I as a translator choose from words and phrases (or come up with new ones) that I already know or could possibly create. In my particular case of translating from native to foreign language, my sense of English would be able to recognise and translate what it already knows within narrower limits, as Buzelin rightly notes, "[w]hether with texts from their own culture or with foreign texts, translators apply their own structures and preconceptions and translate what they have been able to recognise, what they already know" (49). Hence I am faced with a double dilemma: limited knowledge exacerbated by native-language preconceptions. The problem is further intensified by the element of collectivism — i.e., working with a native-English-speaking editor (John Woodsworth).

This research will address the question of the agents of translation, especially in the case of the opening line of Anatoly Nazirov's *Zarathustra* and word-coinages. As Buzelin points out, the process of translation is important and complex (51–52) and must be studied from the point of view of the agents involved in the translation process (52), in accordance with Buzelin's definition of translation as "a dynamic process... involving the confrontation of different points of view" (54). In other words, my translation variants will have to be confronted by my editor's suggestions, so as to determine to what degree my translation has been domesticated.

At the centre of this research lies hidden the question whether the translator can master a foreign language to the point of being capable of translating a poetic text into it from his native tongue — a very challenging task, indeed — with the same (or similar) quality he could have achieved in translating in the opposite direction. This will require further investigation and analysis of particular examples from *Zarathustra*.

3. Word-coinages

In his treatise *Translating Greek Orations into Latin,* Cicero deals with a particular aspect of translation — namely, the coining of new words by analogy with a fair amount of sense appropriateness. One may already notice that making new words in the target language is a possibility that may enrich not only the text of the original (now in its translated form) but also the target language itself. However, it is quite important to maintain a sense of appropriate meaningfulness, and that should be understood as new words simply making sense (a basic communicative act) to native speakers of the target language. It is expected that a newly coined word would broaden the meaning of word-components which have never hitherto been put together in a semantically valid collocation. The combination of word-components in a coinage (as a solid combination of words and morphemes formed on the basis of already existing word-formation patterns and bearing sufficient transparency of meaning) will, assuming the admissibility of a certain collocation, effectively produce a desired meaning redefining or creating an intended idea. At the same time, however, one must bear in mind the degree of departure from the original text. When coining new words by analogy or otherwise, one may unwittingly overdo in terms of the original meaning and produce a slightly or even significantly better or worse (or, simply, quite off-track) translation, yet capturing the overall idea of the original.

In this regard, since A.E. Nazirov's *Zarathustra* abounds in new coinages in the Russian, it immediately presents difficulties for the translator for several reasons. First, if analogy is utilised, the English translation may result in awkwardness. So in this case, the translator is advised to abstain from excessive literalness in his task. Another option would be to ignore the new coinage in the original text and convey it in standard English. While this would certainly diminish the expressive weight of the original Russian, it would at the same time prevent the English translation from sounding inappropriate to the anglophone reader.

One might also opt for a third way of rendering a coinage — not by analogy but by similarity, but here certain conditions would have to be met. First and foremost, it is the availability in the target language of possible variants of word-collocations that would sound appropriate to the native English ear. The degree of necessity of rendering the text by similar coinages would be another factor to take into account. Whether the coinage would necessarily solve or otherwise aid the task of the translator to convey the spirit of the original, or whether it would suffice to circumvent any or all Russian coinages in *Zarathustra* and come up with alternatives on the other linguistic levels (e.g. syntactical or lexical) as to compensate for the lack of coinages in the target text, or totally disregard any or all newly made words in the original is the question that presses itself into the mind of the translator every time he sets himself to translate *Zarathustra*.

An example from the poem of a coinage would be the word приозёрность (*priozernost'*) in the following line:

И мгла, как игла, прилегла в приозёрность (3)

which literally conveys 'near-the-lakeness', i.e., an area that surrounds and includes a lake, and not just any lake but the lake in the village of Priozernoe (Приозёрное) where I was born and raised, and where the poet used to visit in the summer. And one time the poet returned to the village after a ten-year absence, just like the character Zarathustra in the introduction to the poem:

С восходом узорной зари сходит с горы
Заратустра к холодному озеру,
Десятилетье назад оставленному. (3)

As the morning dawn ascends, down the mountain descends
Zarathustra towards the cold lake in the valley
That he had to abandon ten long years ago.

The coinage broadly hints at that particular lake in the village of Priozernoe, and here the translator must be familiar with the personal experiences of the poet. Not only that, but the poet has also written an entire poem devoted to that particular village. Its original title "Priozernoe" was replaced by "Landscape" in publication, as there is hardly a person who knows that village except those who live there or who have ties with it. But the significance of the coinage in question remains important to the original and the poet's personal experiences. To grasp that, one only needs to read the entire poem about this village:

ПЕЙЗАЖ	LANDSCAPE
При озёрах светлое селенье С кучерявой зеленью садов И с весёлой россыпью домов, Что жуют варенья и соленья.	Near the lakes there is a white-bright village With green gardens' curly locks uncombed, With a cheerful scattering of homes, Chewing jam and pickles from their tillage.
На лугу в пруду лягушек хор Исполняет песенки степные, И собаки – жители земные – Затевают скорый разговор,	In a meadow pond a chorus of frogs Well performs their steppe songs in the valleys While fast dialogues are struck in alleys By their earthly dwellers — i.e., dogs.
Не тревожа томных глаз коровы, Приютивших вечную печаль... В зной душа набросить тучу-шаль На литые небеса готова.	This does not affect the languid heifer's Eyes that harbour an eternal woe. In the heat my heart is fit to throw Cloth-like clouds o'er hot and melting heavens.
(from *A Poet's Gallery* II, 24)	(from *A Poet's Gallery* II, 25, *my translation*)

Despite the importance of the coinage, its literal (specifically word-for-word and morpheme-for-morpheme) translation of *pri-ozer-nost'* (hyphenated for visual clarity), as *near-the-lake-ness* is not permissible in the target language, either on the word or morpheme level; besides, it completely loses its poetics. The domesticated version suggested by my editor dominates:

And gloom, like a harpoon, looms piercing the pondside

The lakeside or pondside are the best domesticated equivalences for the *priozernost'* and certainly outshine the near-the-lakeness, or the lakeness, which would be a very literal translation of the Russian coinage. Domestication must prevail, and in this particular case, my editor's suggestion takes precedence.

4. Alliteration and Assonance

The Latin and Greek grammarian Aulus Gellius (also known by the corruption 'Agellius' in the Middle Ages) stands in favour of translational creativity, defending Virgil's free Latin translations from Homer's Greek, for example. Virgil, when translating into Latin, omitted many Greek culturally embedded expressions and substituted for them no less successful and powerful words having "almost more charming and graceful effects" (Robinson 20) in the target language. In his treatise "On the Importance of Avoiding Strict Literalness" from *Attic Nights*, Gellius insists "that we should not strive to render every single word with exact literalness. For many things lose their charm if they are transplanted too forcibly — unwillingly, as it were, and reluctantly" (Robinson 20 – 21). In other words, Gellius follows this simple rule in judgement about translation, namely, that one should leave out certain things while rendering others in their stead. This compensative approach,[2] as I would term it, seemingly allows for a possibility of solving problems in translation, that is, whatever presents itself as untranslatable to the translator at first glance might be totally disregarded but then counterbalanced by the expansion of the meaning of other no less important words or phrases in the text. This points to a creative replacement technique that any literary translator should possess and use at his or her discretion as appropriate.

It follows that the above approach might be especially applicable in the case of *Zarathustra*, which is rife with words, phrases and even sentence structures (a distinctive feature of this poet) not only deeply rooted in Russian culture but also stemming directly from the poet's originality intertwined with his personal life experiences. While we cannot leave out a good portion of the Russian textual meaning, neither can we abandon the poet's experiences of reality implicit in the narrative and at times resounding through Zarathustra's silent speaking. The following question should be raised: do we translate the poem, or do we translate the feelings and emotions of the poet intertwined with those of his literary hero?

Translation of feelings and emotions – and *Zarathustra* is highly emotionally charged as a work of art, the emotive aspect is at the forefront of the poem – is impossible through merely literal translation of words and phrases, especially if there is a danger of them resulting in awkwardness, as previously explored in the Cicero example. But unearthing hidden emphatic words in the target language – that may

---

2 See further Л.С. Бархударов «Язык и перевод». Москва: Международные отношения, 1975. [L.S. Barkhudarov *Yazyk i perevod*. Moskva: Mezhdunarodnye otnosheniya, 1975]

invoke in the reader associations with his or her personal life-experiences in his mother-tongue culture — is a psychological attempt of the translator (who is at the same time trying to remain faithful to the source text) at penetrating the reader's mind to touch the heart of the reader and compel him or her to self-criticism. This is the true task of the philosopher: to show what it is like to deal with oneself on one's own. So, the translator performs not only the role of a translator as such, but also that of a philosopher who has an acute psychological perception of the movements of the anglophone soul.

The above points to the fact that the translator is positioned not only between two cultures and two languages but also between two presumably different life-experiences — that of the Russian author and that of the English reader. Moreover, not only may life-experiences differ from person to person within one particular culture (native or foreign) but also between the cultures within the latter. This even further complicates the task of the translator (though this is not the focus of our discussion). In the first place, in order for the poet to be understood, the reader of the original has to acquaint him- or herself with the author as closely as possible. Such familiarisation already presupposes knowledge of and acquaintance with Friedrich Nietzsche's philosophical and philological background, his autobiography and most personal book, as he himself calls it, *Thus Spoke Zarathustra*. Since Anatoly Nazirov's poem is inspired by Nietzsche's work, it certainly echoes its tone and ideas, but at the same time contributes a significant original addition thereto, totally transforming the poetic-prosaic German into a wholly poetic Russian tongue. The challenge to the translator is to transform the poetic Russian into poetic English, taking into account the author's experience of the peculiarities of the Russian language. This will be pursued further below.

The philosophical poem *Zarathustra* was written to be read aloud, just like Homer's original Greek texts. The role of sound is to emphasise the ideas in the poem. Moreover, thought and sound must perfectly match. In "A Defence of Poetry" Percy Bysshe Shelley writes on the importance of sound and thought connections in poetry: "Sounds as well as thoughts have relations both between each other and towards that which they represent, and a perception of the order of these relations has always been found connected with a perception of the order of the relations of thought" (Levefer 56). The body of the poem is composed of alliteration and assonance, along with expressive words and sentence structures. The words resound when voiced and play on the strings of the soul. But alliteration and assonance often defy translation. So, in the case of the latter occurrence, substitutions for alliterated words and/or phrases and other word-plays in the original Russian should be resorted to and attempted in other parts of the text as appropriate to the target language. This context also takes account of the personal experiences of the anglophone reader, who may not have already encountered acoustically similar or identical words with different meanings. Here the originality of the translator comes into play (not, however, without the author's own pattern) for such words, when used alongside one another in a semantically valid combination, may be linked through one common and interchangeable meaning.

Note, for example that the 'lie' of the serpent can mean either 'lying on the ground' or 'lying as deception'; such duplicity is completely characteristic of the serpent within the context of the introduction to *Zarathustra*. In an e-mail to my editor, I expressed my concern about the difficulty of translating some words in the poem:

> Attached I am sending you a piece of my translation of the long poem *Zarathustra* by A. Nazirov based on *Thus Spake Zarathustra* by F. Nietzsche. I have spent many years translating (or trying to translate) it and have come up with many versions of it. While I am more or less satisfied with my translation of the rest of the poem, I am completely frustrated with my translation of the beginning of the poem (first 40 lines). These introduction lines give me no rest; I cannot get my mind around how to translate it, and there are several reasons for it. The original is blank verse, free verse, rhymed verse, internal rhymes, metric verse, alliterated verse plus assonance – all combined, to say nothing of the images, culture, philosophy, etc.
>
> Example:

> "Ya orlom gor dostig, zmeey dumy rastil
> Iz meda i yada tumannoy mudrosti"
>
> Where you find: "gor dostig" (reached mountains) sounds as "gordosti" (pride) "dumy rastil" (I grew up my thoughts) as "mudrosti" ("MUD" is "DUM(y)" [thought(s)] in reverse).
>
> Another example:
>
> "Vidit — roshsha slepa, slyshit — ropshshet tropa"
>
> You can hear this sound cluster "Tr": "VidiT – Roshsha"; "slyshiT – Ropshshet" plus "TRopa."
>
> There is always something in every line, which makes the poem difficult to translate. Apart from these difficulties, I can hardly put words together for them to make a certain rhythm in a certain context. It defies my translation abilities. I've made a simple, so to speak, translation of it, prosaic, maybe, at times, it may sound poetic, but in general, I am not happy with it at all. So, maybe, you could give me a hint how to cope with this piece of poetry.

My editor's response was as follows:

> With certain poems a play on words can be sometimes too strong and too language-specific to convey in another language. I've come across these before — including ones I myself have written in Russian. In such cases one can only come as close as possible and give the reader some idea (in a footnote) as to what the Russian play on words is about. That's my initial reaction to the examples you give, but I look forward to examining this problem more closely when I have time.

The problem as described above is clear. I had to find words in the English that would imitate alliteration and assonance in the Russian original. And I think I did in the second example:

Видит — роща слепа, слышит — ропщет тропа (3)
(*Literally:* he sees the grove is blind; he hears the trail grumbling)
He sees the sightless trees, he hears the trail bewailing

For if one considers these sound clusters as compensating for the loss of the repetitive Russian [tr] and [sch] sounds in the translation, then one shares the idea that translation is possible through domestication: [sees], [-less], [trees], and even, though tenuously, [hears] plus [tr]ees and [tr]ail, and tr[ail] and bew[ail]ing.

As to the first example, only my resort to and much reliance on the domesticating process (along with my editor's suggestion) saved my translation, though I do not exclude the possibility of inserting a footnote explaining to the reader the specificities of the original:

Я орлом гор достиг, змеёй думы растил
Из мёда и яда туманной мудрости (3)
(Literally:
I reached the mountains like an eagle,
                        grew up my thoughts like a serpent
From the honey and poison of foggy wisdom)

I pried from an eagle's high and a serpent's lie
From honey hocks and toxins of misty wit

Indeed, "pried" now sounds as pride and connotes flight as *dostig* (reached) in the Russian, but "serpent's lie" has the double meaning: *lying* on the ground or *lying* as speaking falsely (or perhaps in a round-about way as wisely), which might hint at wisdom; this is not to say that wisdom is lying, but oftentimes wisdom is belied, for truth hurts.

As much as I would want as a translator to preserve the literalness of the Russian original, I realise that, try as I might, it would be utterly impossible to render the ambiguous Russian alliterations, assonances and other word-plays while at the same time making philosophical sense in the specific context. This is simply due to the incompatibility of Russian and English in word-composition and word combination. The literalness would be sacrificed and one would be obliged to introduce a lengthy translator's footnote explaining what is untranslatable in the original. Such an addition to the translation is helpful, as it sheds more light on the poet's originality as well as on the peculiar flexibility of the Russian language. However, footnoting may be considered by some as a lack of the translator's skill or even a failure on his part to cope with the intricacies of the language of the poem. Nevertheless, this should not discourage the translator or the reader but on the contrary stimulate the interest of anglophone readers in a language different from theirs and thus offer new possibilities of looking at the world through the prism of another language and culture. A fair interchange of language and culture represents neither loss nor failure.

5. Incommensurability of Russian and English

Since language is regarded culturally determined, according to both Jacques Derrida and Gayatri Chakravorty Spivak ("Translation as Culture"), there lies a wide cultural gap between Russian and English and this may find its confirmation in the following example. Russian *diminutive words* are for the most part untranslatable in English. Diminutive words are personal, intimate expressions of one's feelings, emotions, attitude toward a person or object; they are formed simply by adding diminutive suffixes to regular words.

This is not to say that English completely lacks such a phenomenon. For example, 'starlet'[3] would be a reference to a little star and bear connotations of the personal attitude of the speaker. It is noteworthy that the diminutive suffix *-let* in English is pretty much non-productive, i.e., it is very rarely used in new word-combinations. So, in contrast to Russian, diminutive forms are not a widespread phenomenon in English language and culture. Furthermore, most English words function to convey information rather than the speaker's emotions, whereas in Russian diminutive words, in combination with the flexibility of language structure, do not *inform* so much as *pour out* the speaker's heart to the listener.

---

3 Editor's note: 'starlet' is used (quite commonly) as a diminutive of 'star', but almost exclusively in the Hollywood sense and only for young female actresses or performers on their way to being a star (a 'star' can be either male or female but a 'starlet' is nearly always female). The word 'starlet' is rarely used in the astronomical sense (perhaps occasionally in old-fashioned poetry).

Nazirov's poem *Zarathustra* does not bypass either the use of diminutive words or the flexibility of Russian language structure. Indeed, diminution is an integral part of the poem. As previously stated, *-let* is adaptable to few words beyond *starlet*. The following example from the poem will demonstrate this. The Russian word *лужайка* (23) is basically translated as "meadow", but in this particular context it could be rendered literally as "a little meadow", and not just "meadow", which would be simply informative without reference to its size and, more importantly, to the poet's attitude towards the object of description.

In his article "How to Translate Well From One Language to Another", Etienne Dolet, a French translator who was wrongly convicted and executed by the church for mistranslating a Latin text into French to make it sound as "that there is nothing after death" (Robinson 95), discusses a very important principle which, in my judgement, is central to the translation of Nazirov's *Zarathustra*. He raises the issue of the translator having "a perfect familiarity with the language of the author being translated, as well as equal facility with the language into which the former is translating" (Robinson 96). He indicates a possible incongruity between the source and target languages in terms of their word stock. One of the languages involved in a translation process may have a richer vocabulary than the other and this presents difficulties to the translator, who must make a choice as to either borrow words from the source language or find and use ordinary, common words in the target language, or both.

Both Russian and English are highly developed languages and both have rich vocabularies. English is notable for its polysemy. One word — for example *make* (especially as a phrasal verb, e.g. *make up, make out, make away* etc.), — may have over a hundred meanings quite unrelated to its original meaning. The Russian language is much less polysemantic, and uses different words for what may be expressed by one (and the same) word in English. But how do we translate the Russian *светило* referencing the sun in the following lines from *Zarathustra*?

Чтобы сталось, светило, со счастьем твоим,
Если б ты никому никогда не светило? (3)

Literally *светило* (svetilo) as a noun (as opposed to *светило* as the past tense (third person, singular, neuter) of *светить* (to shine): Zarathustra playfully challenges the function *светить* (to shine) of *светило* (the sun) in his address to the heavenly body) means something or somebody that lights, or shines, or illumines, with a poetical touch to it. We are of course aware of the English words *star* and *orb* which sound poetical in reference to the sun. Why is there laid so much importance on the sun in the original poem? Because the sun is a symbol of wisdom and Zarathustra is a protagonist of wisdom. To convey the thought that the sun is not just a star, an orb or an eye but primarily an agent of wisdom, the translator might be tempted to choose human-reference terms such as lighter or *illuminer* But because there are certain linguistic limitations — in any language, not only in English — rendering *светило* as *lighter* will not make much (poetical) sense but produce a humoristic effect, especially by inducing associations with a certain mechanical device. So the poetical *orb* is rather preferred:

> Your euphoria, Orb, it would not be absorbed and gone
> If your orbit never shone for anyone?

Another problem described in Dolet's text is subservient adherence to the original arrangement of words, word-combinations and sentence structures, as if to convey the spirit of the original but, unsurprisingly, resulting in misconstruing the meaning and intentions of the author. It would be quite legitimate, for example to make a word-for-word translation of the following two lines in Nazirov's *Zarathustra*:

> Горят у зари уста, остыв, острыми
> Глазами в озеро уставленной. (3)

as:

> The lips of dawn are burning (aglow), getting cold, with her sharp
> Eyes staring into the lake.

But the first half of the first line in the original is supposed to be alliterative, to echo the name "Zarathustra": *Goryat <u>u zari usta</u>*.

Indeed, *u zari usta* does sound like *Zarathustra* in the Russian. The appearance of Zarathustra — literally *zara* (dawn) + *astra* (star) is thus associated with the ascending of the morning star. The English alliterative equivalent that I was able to come up with is *the illustrious star* which has at least a partial acoustic resemblance to the name *Zarathustra*. But the original meaning is lost here. To compensate for the loss, I have moved this wonderful figure of speech of the poet's to the end of the sentence on the next line and rearranged the sentence structure as follows:

> The illustrious star arises; the dawn's sharp eyes
> Staring at the lake and her lips aglow.

It is plain to see that a different word order in this case is vital to the sentence, while preserving the original sentence structure would suggest the translator is ignorant of the language, meaning and intentions of the poet. Fortunately, we found a way around it. Yet my editor (who is also a Russian-to-English literary translator) recommended that I should reverse the order of "Arises the illustrious star" to meet the English language norms. Initially I thought that it would be best to preserve the Russian predicate-subject word order in the opening line in order to emphasise the action of the agent rather than the agent himself. Nietzsche was the first to say that there is no doer behind the action — a very important step that charted a new way in philosophy for the following twentieth and twenty-first centuries up to the present moment. Subjectivity has become decentred. Action (especially the potentiality thereof) is what now matters. The question of Being is raised by Martin Heidegger. Dispersal of meaning is given voice through Jacques Derrida, resulting in the untranslatability of text as culture. Otherwise, my translation would have sounded originally as follows:

> Arises the illustrious star...

To a native English speaker such as my editor, this word order seemed a bit unnatural in English, hence his suggestion will prevail over my translation variant. As a non-native speaker of English I cannot feel this unnaturalness in its full scope, but I comprehend it with my mind, which means that I have learned the proper grammar rules to follow without perhaps ever breaking them. But to understand those rules, the foreign mind, as mine is with respect to English, has a different sensitivity to what is not innate in it. One may even go so far as to call it stiff and rigid. Yet it is also possible for the flexibility of the Russian language to assert itself and influence foreign patterns by transforming and adapting them to itself. In such a case the subject-predicate word order would be reversed, after the pattern of the original Russian sentence structure. Yet, on the other hand, one could also say that no rule can be entirely understood before one actually breaks it, and this often happens with beginners in a language.

Early modern English poetry, however, did allow for departures from standard grammar rules; they might have been still lax in those times, yet not without the influence upon late modern and contemporary English. Inversion is still acceptable if it is contextually justified. And whether this particular example from Zarathustra is worthy of being admitted for consideration as one of those justifiable contexts, where inversion gives a significant positive twist to the majesty of the text, such a decision is left up to the subjective interpretation of the reader. The good thing about it is that the subject-predicate word order, as it stands, makes for an internal rhyme: "The illustrious star <u>arises</u>; the dawn's sharp <u>eyes,</u> ..." and may thus be considered 'domesticated'.

Conclusion

I would like to conclude my paper by citing the new approaches to translation offered by John Dryden, the first translation theorist in the Western history of translation. In his article "The Three Types of Translation" he discusses metaphrase, paraphrase and imitation. In an another article, "Steering Between Two Extremes", he opts to work "betwixt the two extremes of paraphrase and literal translation" (Robinson 174); for him words are a dress for poetry without which it loses its beauty. John Dryden, on the whole, considers the main task of the translator not only to render the meaning as such but also to find, in the target language, words and figures of speech (where the poet's own words or idioms make little or no sense in a literal translation) such as would most closely reflect the original — words or phrases that the poet himself might have used were he to write in

English (assuming that were possible to know). This may be considered the most revolutionary approach ever taken to translation since antiquity.

Following John Dryden, to find suitable words to translate Nazirov's complex philosophical poem *Zarathustra* has been, as the above analysis shows, quite a labour. I have had to take into account not only the philosophical weight of meaning but also the loftiness of the poet's unique and masterful poetic style. The difficulty here lies in a perfect combination of both, so as not to privilege philosophy over poetry or poetry over philosophy, for injustice should not be done to either, but to strike an *aurea mediocritas*, a creative *golden mean*. Like Dryden, as the translator of Nazirov's *Zarathustra* — *couldn't he use simpler language and thoughts when he was writing this poem! (though if he did, to be sure, it would not have become the centre of our attention)* — I could not allow myself to imitate it, varying the meaning or words in such a manner as to entirely re-create the poem, to make it solely my own. It *must* be shared, for certain. Imitation is useful as practice of one's poetic genius and should sometimes be resorted to in search of new thoughts and ideas ripe and juicy to sweeten the bitter poison of the philosophical sense, one that Nazirov, after Nietzsche, so skilfully conveys to the reader — the cup of bitter-sweet poison that humanity must drink in order to become an 'over-humanity'.

Further, I note Dryden saying that he borrowed many words from Latin into English, thus enriching the vocabulary of the recipient language. In my judgement, however, I could not be a proponent of doing as he had done for the following reasons.

First, russifying the English language could be taken as an indicator of my unsuccessful attempts at translation. On the other hand, making my translation as English-sounding as possible, as natural as the original ideas and language could allow, would have put me on a par with a native English speaker. Hence I realise at once that there has been a learning component involved here. To rebut my own self-accusation of striving to achieve native language competence through translation from native to foreign language — though it may be a justifiably valid reason as well, perhaps the strongest stimulus I have ever had in my life as far as my creative work is concerned — I have resolved to bequeath a part of Russian culture and language to my

English audience, but in such a way as to make my gift as their own. That is, the language used in the translation must be English on every possible level: idioms, where necessary; assonances and alliterations, through imitating the sound of the original Russian words, where possible; rhythm and rhyme structures identical with or resembling those of the original, and so on and so forth. Only when all of these are dealt with in translation can the translation be called by its own name. The difficulty here is this golden mean: to make almost a literal translation such that it may sound just like any original English text, with ease and grace, to render complex yet vivid Russian philosophical-poetical images into similar English ones, to transfuse the Russian spirit of the original and Nazirov's wisdom through every minute detail of every word and line into solid, monolithic English verse and culture — in short, to make English feel and sound like at home. This not only strikes a balance between the original and the target, between the native and the foreign, but also tips the scale towards what is more natural-sounding in the target language and culture, where what is foreign to me (English) becomes native to my translation, and what is foreign to the English audience (the Russian original) becomes *dom*-esticated (Latin *domus* or Russian *dom* = house/home). Translation as domestication emancipates itself from the original.

In general, the following inferences can be drawn from the above analysis of my translation of Anatoly Nazirov's *Zarathustra*:

1. A translator who is sufficiently proficient in the Russian language and whose native language (i.e., a language learnt from infancy), as in my editor's case, is English– can in most cases make a better translation from the Russian to English than a non-native speaker of the target language;

2. Yet, on the other hand, a native speaker of the source language can have a better understanding and feel of the Russian original and give attention to certain particulars of the text in an attempt to render them into English, rather than leaving them out;

3. Even if a translator such as in my case can make both linguistically and poetically acceptable rendition of the original Russian into English, the translation will come out more Russian- than English-sounding — as opposed to a more English- than Russian-sounding translation made by a native speaker of the target language;

4. The inference I have just drawn serves as a stimulus to strike a balance between the original and the target, the foreign and the native language, in my translation learning process, in my progress from the source to the target language, from my native Russian Self to my English Other self;

5. Once I find myself at the golden mean between Russian and English, a certain sacrifice of Russianness still present in my translation will be necessary in order to further domesticate the original, as a continuation of my learning progress on the path to second-language acquisition through translation from my native Russian to my non-native English.

I would like to encourage those, who, like myself, are involved in translating challenging works from their native to a foreign language and find it difficult or even impossible to pass through the transparent wall that separates them from the foreign target language and through which they can see it, but cannot approach and touch it, as it were, by citing my editor's comments as a way of confirmation that successful attempts have already been made:

> And I would say to you in return: DON'T LOSE HOPE! You seem to have a very good command of English, certainly in writing prose, but translating literature, especially poetry, into other than one's native language is one of the most challenging translation tasks one can attempt — witness my own poor attempts to translate poetry into Russian (thank you very much for your comments on those, by the way). The only thing harder than that to do is translating humour into a language other than your own. And the wall you speak of is more porous than you think — you've already managed to puncture quite a few holes in it! :-)
>
> So do keep on with it – your attempts are very good, and you will get better with practice. I might suggest reading already published translations of Russian authors in English – as many as you can find, and compare them with the original. That will give you (over time) a better idea of what is acceptable in translation...

Ничего, мой друг! Основу Вы уже положили. Стройте на ней.

(Never mind, my friend! You have already laid the foundation. Now build on it. – *my translation from the Russian*)

There is just a little bit more to include in my conclusion, and paradoxically it is this: when I indeed break through the wall that, like an obstacle, stands in my way between Russian and English, created by these two languages (i.e., *Russian holding me back* — hence the russification of English, and *English not admitting me* — hence the original sense is not conveyed by my limited English) as I tread along the trail from the native language and culture that I am, to the foreign language and culture that I yet am not, then I as the Self and my translation as my Other self can unhesitatingly be called domesticated.

Works Cited

Benjamin, Walter. *Illuminations*, trans. Harry Zohn. Ed. Hannah Arendt. New York: Schocken Books, 1968.

Buzelin, Hélène. "Translation Studies, Ethnography and the Production of Knowledge." Ed. Paul St-Pierre and Prafulla C. Kar. *In Translation – Reflections, Refractions, Transformations*. Amsterdam/Philadelphia: John Benjamins Publishing Company, 2007. 39 – 56. Web. 28 February 2010.

Lefevere, André, and Susan Bassnett. Ed. *Translation, History, Culture: A Source Book*. London and New York: Routledge, 1992. Web. 28 February 2010.

Nazirov, Anatoly. *A Poet's Gallery*. Book II, trans. Ivan Zhavoronkov. Toronto: 2009.

____. *"Заратустра" (по мотивам произведения Ф. Ницше "Так говорил Заратустра"). Философская поэма. Санкт-Петербург – 1993)* [Zarathustra (po motivam proizvedeniya F. Nietzsche "Tak govoril Zaratustra") Filosofskaya poema], St-Petersburg: Tekhpribor, 1993.

Nietzsche, Friedrich. *The Gay Science*, trans. Walter Kaufmann. New York: Random House, 1974.

Robinson, Douglas, ed. *Western Translation Theory*. Manchester: St. Jerome Publishing, 1997.

Venuti, Lawrence. "Translation, Community and Utopia." *The Translation Studies Reader*. Ed. Lawrence Venuti. London: New York Taylor & Francis · Routledge, 2000. 468 – 488. Web. 28 February 2010.

СТИХИ
POEMS

ЛЕС ПОЭЗИИ

*Посвящается памяти
поэта А.А. Шевелёва*

Налиты почками слова
На ветках дерева-стиха,
Поэмы рощами, дубравами,
Кустарниками, травами
Волнуются, живут,
А их герои птицами -
Скворцами и синицами,
На ветках гнёзда вьют.
Шумят леса поэзии,
О коей и не грезили
Лесничие-сычи,
И совы толстосумые,
И филины заумные,
И ссыльные грачи.
Бывает, в дни засушья
Стоят леса, заслушавшись
Напевами дубов -
Классических стихов,
Они живут степенные,
Проверенные временем
Умельцы волшебства.
И льют дожди фантазии
На лес и степь Евразии,
И прорастает заново
Зелёная листва.

IN THE WOOD OF POETRY

*Dedicated to the memory
of the poet A.A. Shevelev*

Like bursting buds, there burgeon words
On branches of the tree of verse.
Poems, like thickets, coppices,
Grasses and bushy lattices
Flourish and take no rest;
Their heroes, like bird-warriors,
Like starlings, titmice, gloriously
Keep busy building nests.
The leafy wood of poetry
Is murmuring alluringly,
Of whose diffusing scent
The exiled rooks and foresters,
Wise eagle owls, in loneliness
Have never even dreamt.
In times of weather hot and dry
The oak-trees, classics, versify:
The forest gets immersed
In listening to their verse, –
The skilled magicians, unperplexed,
Time-tested, steady and relaxed –
So do they live and reign.
When raindrops fall in fantasy,
Intoxication, ecstasy,
On woods and steppes Eurasian,
New leaves appear again.

ГУДОК

До сих пор мне не ведомо средство,
Чтобы душу пронзило сильней,
Чем гудок из далёкого детства –
Он и ныне мне снится во сне...

После смерти «отца всех народов»
Пережили весну не легко
И под гул обновлённой природы
Сели мы на речной пароход.

Чтобы в трюм не спускались мы – дети,
Нас пугали: «Там страшный медведь».
Облаками текла на рассвете
Прямо в реку небесная твердь.

Верба грустно стояла у дома,
Молчаливо внимая ручьям.
Солнце смело лучами-соломой
Пило влагу, о неге крича.

ЮНОСТЬ

Расцветает весной в полнолуние
Юность тайными грёзами втуне и
Покрывается ранними ранами,
Прорывается рваными гранями
Как алмазными в море руинами –
Затаёнными талыми льдинами:
Неотлаженными, неотделанными
Микеланджелами и Роденами.

THE SHIP'S BLAST

I have known nothing else in existence
To have pierced my heart ever so deep
As the ship's blast from childhood so distant,
That I hear even now, in my sleep.

When "the father of all of the nations"
Died that spring we then barely survived.
Soon we boarded a steamboat, elated,
To the sweet sounds of nature, revived.

We were scared off the hold, kids so curious:
"There's a terrible bear down inside".
As we sailed on, the sky-gold so furious
Melted down in the blue rivertide.

Just beside our own home stood a willow
Listening, quiet, to the stream in deep grief.
And the sun with its bright straw-rays freely
Drinking water would cry with relief.

YOUTH

When the full moon in spring looms ferociously,
Youth's once hidden dreams bloom precociously,
All in premature wounds opened jaggedly,
Bursting into keen edges, torn raggedly,
Like diamonds 'neath seas breaking violently,
Like ice-bergs, well hid, melting silently,
Rough, unruly, rebellious and dangerous,
Like Rodins or even Michelangelos.

О СЕБЕ

Посудить пособи, Господи,
О себе, как об особи.
Не родился, не рос в цепи,
Душу вёз, как обоз в степи.
И летят дни мои россыпью
И то яд, а то росы пьют.
А то вьют гнездо птицей певчею.
Коль взорвут звездой, станет легче ль им?
Было б гнёзд, как звёзд, поди,
Без меня, было б рос пуды.
Проследи, посуди, Господи:
Посреди поля роз – один.

***

Букету полевых цветов
Поведать боль свою готов,
И лепет спелых лепестков
Ответит веянием стихов.

***

Моим мечтам даримая,
Ты проходила мимо их.
Ты для меня, что жизнь моя,
Прожитая другими.

ABOUT MYSELF

Let me ask, O my Lord, your assistance
To now ponder my very existence.
I was not born or raised in thick chains;
My own heart weighed me down on the plains;
Now my days fly to pieces, subdued;
First a poison they drink, then sip dew,
Then, like songbirds, they build up their nests.
If they burst just like stars, would they rest?
If nests many as stars there could be,
There'd be thousands of dew-drops like me.
See, O Lord, into what I have grown:
Midst the rose field I stand all alone.

***

My heartache I would gladly nurse
As I with fair field flowers converse.
Their blooms will in return disperse
A wafting scent inspiring verse.

***

You have been passing by my dreams,
My cherished dreams of you alone.
You are just like my life to me,
My life that I have never owned.

***

Ты в детстве в куклы не играла,
Игрушки в руки не брала,
Ты их упорно отвергала -
Меня отчаянно ждала.
Сейчас нечаянно играй
Моей потерею сознанья,
Играй у двери мирозданья,
Открытой в рай.

***

Я вдохнулся в слова -
Только провод сгорел,
Телефонная трубка расплавлена.
И с утра на заре
Во хмелю голова
И сердечная рана подпалена.

***

Обо мне вспоминаешь редко,
Словно сытый о чёрством хлебе,
Как в солнечный день о зонтике,
При светлом безоблачном небе.
Обо мне вспоминаешь редко,
Как папуас об экзотике
Таинственной знойной Африки.
Обо мне вспоминаешь редко.
И дело не в этике, тактике,
Диалектике и дидактике.
А просто в твоём характере:
Для жизни в другой галактике
Проходишь межзвёздную практику.

***

You, as a little girl, wouldn't play ever
With your own doll or teddy bear.
And casting aside your toys forever
You waited for me in despair.
Play now – as carefree in elation –
On my lost mind, before my eyes.
Play at the door of all creation,
In paradise.

***

I breathed upon my words,
Only the telephone wire burned
And the receiver melted immediately.
As the bright morning dawns,
I feel drunk, dizzy, worn,
And my heart-wound's sore pain seared up vehemently.

***

You remember me but only rarely
As the sated stale bread would not treasure,
As you would rarely remember a brolly
When the sky is unclouded and azure.
You remember me but only rarely
As a Papuan would the Exotica
In mysterious, sun-hardened Africa.
You remember me but only rarely,
And the reason's not ethics or tactics,
Dialectics, or even didactics,
But it's all just because of your character.
It's to live in a far-away galaxy
That you midst the stars have been practising.

***

Во время таянья снегов
Закралась тайная тревога,
И тишиной твоих шагов
Дышала дальняя дорога.

Осадки горечи стихов
Ещё бродили хмелем ранним,
Остатки запаха духов
Ещё томили старой раной.

***

Без тебя мне май -
Не цветущий край:
Как верблюжий куст
Для ягнёнка пуст,

Так и мне не мил
Солнца вешний пыл,
Как полям леса
Без шумливых птиц,

Как ребёнку сад
Без родимых лиц.
Без тебя мне май -
Лучше жизнь сломай.

***

Для чего мне цветы на поляне,
Беспризорная песня в лесу,
Если ходишь, как будто в тумане,
Принимая за слёзы росу?

Что мне лето в сиянии света,
Что мне радость от солнечных сосен?
Если нет от тебя ответа,
В моё лето врывается осень.

***

When winter's snows began to melt,
Into my heart there crept a worry.
The distant, breathing roadway felt
Your quiet footsteps' pace, unhurried.

The bitter dregs of verse still brewed,
Like early hops, intoxicating;
And, like an old wound, now renewed,
Your scent remained, excruciating.

***

Spring without you looms
As lands with no blooms,
As is a camel's place
For a lamb to graze,

Like fields without herbs,
Like woods without birds,
Sun's heat without light –
Not my spring's delight,

Like a day-care child
Of his kin deprived.
Spring without you? Why,
I would rather die.

***

Why care I for flowers in meadows
Or some bird-song which wasted appears,
If I'm roaming through dark, misty shadows
While mistaking fresh dew-drops for tears?

Why care I for summer light's splendour,
Why do bright sunlit pines give me pleasure?
If you show no response sweet and tender,
Autumn breaks through my summer sky's azure.

***

То луной лукавой
Смотришь на меня,
То качнёшь оправой
Золотого дня.

Утренняя свежесть
Льётся из души,
Чувственную нежность
Мне не потушить.

Но беги от боли
Пламенных оков
И не слушай более
Ты моих стихов.

ПРОВОЛОКА

Обмотался колючей проволокой,
Пропустил по ней ток электрический,
Чтобы, гладя ладонью шелковой
Меня, как ежа с иголками,
Приходила б ты в ужас панический.

Не пугало меня напряжение
И смерть по своей небрежности.
Боялся я только сожжения
От капли полученной нежности.

***

First you, sly as moonshine,
Spy on me at night,
Then in golden sunshine's
Frame you hold me tight.

With the morning's freshness
Overflows my heart.
Tender feelings, quenchless,
I would fain impart.

But you flee forever
Flaming passion's chains
And no more, not ever,
Hear my sweet refrains.

BARBED WIRE

I wrapped up in barbed wire apprehensively
And put through it high-voltage electricity
So with silken hands stroking me, pensively,
Me – a hedgehog with quills poised defensively,
You would panic with mad eccentricity.

I was not at all frightened of torturing
By high-tension wires in their deadliness.
I was only afraid of the scorchingly
Burning touch of your passionate tenderness.

***

Блаженства суть яви, открой.
К чему идти через страданья?
Как будто в мире есть покой
Помимо твоего дыханья.

К чему скорбеть в краю унылом
По жизни горестной своей?
Как будто есть моя могила
Помимо памяти твоей.

***

Тебе меня немного не хватает,
Как лунной ночи Млечного Пути,
Весенним снегом наша нежность тает,
Надежде помогая прорасти.

Звенящим колокольчиковым полем
В нас говорят минуты забытья.
И, словно подчиняясь высшей воле,
Немую грусть в дыханье затая,

В туманном сновиденье замечаю
Волнующий божественный проект:
Дорога лунная спокойными ночами
В небесный выливается проспект.

***

Reveal the sense of bliss, disclose.
Why should I go through tribulations?
As though on earth there were repose
Apart from your own respirations.

Why should I grieve my fate so twisted
In a land so desolate for me?
As though my grave in earth existed
Apart from your own memory.

***

You miss me only a little in your heart,
Just as the moonlit night – the Milky Way.
Our fondness now like spring snow melts apart,
Helping a hope take root and sprout some day.

The moments of oblivion, as if flowering,
Within us ring, just like a bluebell field.
As if obeying some high will overpowering,
With bated breath my speechless sorrow held,

In misty dream, excited, I envision
The overwhelming plan of God displayed:
The moonlit road winds on through night's soft visions
And then streams out upon the heavenly way.

***

Сказала ты,
Что жить не хочешь,
Что жизнь хохочет
Оскалом лжи,

Что беззащитно,
Хоть и обшито
Сердечко стужей
Твоей тиши.

И как ответят
Мне камни эти,
Что в постаменте
Твоей души?

***

Ты вошла в меня
Хмелем от вина,
Болью от вины,
Вестью седины,
Далью до луны,
Данью тишины.
И до сердца дна
Лишь дошла одна
Глубина твоя.

***

Морякам-поэтам

Во мгле прибой
Ко мне взывал:
"Судьбу отдай!"
По нервам оттепель
Текла,
И в теле музыка
Цвела –
Судьба неистово влекла
В слепую даль.

***

You've told me this:
I want to perish;
For the life I cherish
Lies through her teeth.

My heart defenceless,
Although not senseless,
Wrapped in the tenseness
Of your regard.

What would these boulders
Tell me with boldness,
That rest on coldness
Within your heart?

***

You this life of mine
Filled like heady wine,
Like guilt-pains all day,
Like hair touched with grey,
Like the distant moon,
Like stark quiet's boon.
Only your profound
World its way then found
To my heart's deep ground.

***

To Seamen Poets

The surging surf
Called out to me,
"Give me your life!"
It did on my nerves thaw
And flow,
In me a melody
Did grow,
My heart again would gladly go
To the far unseen.

РАЗМОЛВКА

Живительной влаги, на землю с небес
Вернувшейся строгим парадом, мерцанье
В парадной стоящих,
               у нас
                       вызвало
Звонкое чувство тревоги,
                  грозу предвещавшей.
Во взоре твоем застывала бездонной
                       Вселенной обида.
От вида разверзшихся уст, шевеленьем
Исторгнувших ужас молчанья,
Обрушилась Вечность во мне и меж нами.
Крик молчаливый наполнил
Безмерность тугого пространства.
Мысли скакали Калигулой
Юным и зрелым, нуждаясь
В коррекции полной настройкой рояля.
Карательной влагой на землю с небес
Падали капли камнями на много каратов.

DISENGAGEMENT

The glistening light of refreshing raindrops
Returning to earth, like a hail, from the heavens
Roused in us,
        who stood
                in the grand entrance hall,
A resounding sense of alarm,
                thunderstorm-threatening.
A slur from the bottomless Universe took
                over your gaze.
The look of your lips, as they parted in moving,
Exacting a terrible silence,
Brought down an Eternity in me, between us.
The cry, although silent, still filled
The tenseness of infinite space.
My thoughts like Caligula's rushed,
Both young and mature, still requiring
A piano's inspired fine tuning.
The chastening drops, hastening down from the sky
Pelted the ground in a hail of invaluable gemstones.

ПРИМИРЕНИЕ

Душу сжигала пойманной плазмой
Горечь размолвки, прорваться готовой
Спазмом,
      извергшим всю гордость смиренья.
Гроты амбиций
      сметало картечью упреков,
В зону нейтральных тематик проникших.
Беглый огонь недобитых сарказмов
Выжег окопы последних уловок,
Вызвал постройку моста рефлексии
Над осаждённым пространством гордыни –
В панцирь одетого тела эмоций.
К связкам слова подбирались застенчивым
Штурмом права попиравшего замка,
Споря о праве
      быть первым в ночи новобрачной,
Пронзённой ознобом живого молчанья.

СОГЛАСИЕ

Вакуум хладной раскрытою пастью –
Черной дырою, питаясь Вселенной,
Мне предложил единенье и Вечность:
«Выжди мгновенье и станешь единым
Ты, словно с Богом, в экстазе слиянья».
«Нет», - прозвучало рожденьем
                Вселенной
Из горла, открытого белой дырою,
Аннигилирую плазму амбиций.

RECONCILIATION

The bitterness of disengagement was burning
My soul with plasma now captured, about to rupture
Out through a spasm
      Erupting with all the pride of humility.
The grottos of arrogant pretensions
          Were swept away by buck-shot reproaches
And penetrated a zone of neutral conversation topics.
The fast-running fire of yet unbeaten sarcasms
Burnt out the trenches of traps still remaining,
Called for the building of a bridge of reflection
Across the beleaguered expanse of pride –
Like the body of emotions enclothed in a shell.
There were words being stealthily formed in my throat
Like a shy storm violating the rights of my castle,
Arguing for the right
      To be vocalized first on the newly-weds' night
Impaled by the shivers of living tranquility.

HARMONY

Fed on the Universe through the wide, gaping
Mouth of the black hole, the ever-cold vacuum
Offered me unity, as well as Eternity,
"Wait for a moment and you will become as
One, as with God, in a union of ecstasy".
"No!" came the answer
          through Universe birth-throes,
Out of the throat, like a white hole wide-open,
Annihilating the plasm of arrogance.

ЖЕНЩИНЕ

Бледным ландышем вяло и тускло
Опустилась устало ладонь,
Вы склонились к ней мятою блузкой
С переливами цвета бордо.

Вы напились обманами жизни
И наелись смертями надежд.
Примирились с тоской укоризны
Беззастенчивых с Вами невежд.

Из поклонников только поэтов
Допустили до края души.
Чувства стылые смятым букетом
Перестали в себе ворошить.

Ландыш вещий с пятью лепестками,
Нитью синей питающий жизнь,
Сердце сдерживая корешками,
Удержи ты её, удержи.

***

Ты наговором серебрила
И сны мои и мостовые-зеркала,
И в них запуталась луна
Размазанным кусочком мела.
Какая колдовская сила
Под ноги бросила светило
И размельчила в серебро?
Твои я понял чародейства,
Чудачества и лицедейства,
И магии и волшебства –
В них вижу волю естества.

TO A WOMAN

Like a limp pale-white lily, untwinkled,
Your own hand from fatigue has dropped low.
You have drooped in its wake, your blouse wrinkled,
Iridescent with a tinge of Bordeaux.

You have drunk to the full life's deceptions,
You're fed up with the hopes that are dead,
Reconciled with the angst of rejections
From some shameless know-nothings, ill-bred.

Of your beaus only poets appealing
You've allowed to the edge of your heart.
No longer you stir your cold feeling,
Like a crumpled bouquet, crushed apart.

You prophetic, fine lily, five petals,
You whose azure-blue thread nurtures life,
With your roots that hold up her heart's mettle,
Keep on holding her, holding her tight!

***

You spoke a silver spell away
Upon my dream and mirror-walk,
So, that the moon, like a piece of chalk
Crushed and pale-white, went astray.
What was the magic power that took
And threw the night's orb underfoot
And smashed it into silver pieces?
I've known your foxy fascination,
Your waywardness and simulation,
Your own bewitching magic skills,
In which I well see nature's will.

***

Твои глаза отчаянно молчали,
Искали свой невысказанный глас,
Рассеянный шагами из слогов.
Твои глаза красноречивей
Велеречивых красных языков
Морских сирен, что чаровали
Полубогинь, полубогов,
Оживших в нас...
Я – глаз твоих невысказанный глас.

ВЕСНА

Я увидал издалека,
Как ты, воздушна и легка,
Крылатой феей неземной
Так пропарила надо мной,
Над талым снегом и травой,
Что вместо молока
Коты из лужи дождевой
Лакали облака.

***

Your eyes were keeping desperately silent,
Seeking their very own unspoken voice
Dispersed by steps in syllables at once.
Your eyes – more eloquent and captivating
Than those magniloquent and silver tongues
Of fascinating sirens, once beguiling
The demigoddesses and semi-gods – the ones
That in us rise...
I am the silent speaking of your eyes.

SPRING

Already from afar I saw
You so ethereally soar
O'er me, the grass and the melting snow
Just like a white-winged fairy, so
Divine, unearthly and aglow
That even the cats did drool
While lapping up the clouds below
As milk in a rain pool.

ПЕЙЗАЖ

При озёрах светлое селенье
С кучерявой зеленью садов
И с весёлой россыпью домов,
Что жуют варенья и соленья.

На лугу в пруду лягушек хор
Исполняет песенки степные,
И собаки – жители земные –
Затевают скорый разговор,

Не тревожа томных глаз коровы,
Приютивших вечную печаль...
В зной душа набросить тучу-шаль
На литые небеса готова.

ЭСКИЗ

Алине Мальцевой

Полыханье цветущей полыни
Одурманило воздух полей,
Колыханье поющей калины
Затуманило дух тополей.

И пленение жара в полене
Ожидало паденья в камин,
А томление пара по лени
Оживало оленем шальным.

LANDSCAPE

Near the lakes there is a white-bright village
With green gardens' curly locks uncombed,
With a cheerful scattering of homes,
Chewing jam and pickles from their tillage.

In a meadow pond a chorus of frogs
Well performs their steppe songs in the valleys
While fast dialogues are struck in alleys
By their earthly dwellers – i.e., dogs.

This does not affect the languid heifer's
Eyes that harbour an eternal woe.
In the heat my heart is fit to throw
Cloth-like clouds o'er hot and melting heavens.

SKETCH

To Alina Maltseva

The whole flagrance of blossoming flowers
Has befuddled the earth in the breeze.
While the fragrance of gossiping clovers
Has bemuddled the mirth of the trees.

And the gleam of the log slyly burning
Has survived to now sear in the fire.
While the steam, lazy fog, shyly yearning,
Has revived, like a deer in desire.

СОН

Плутаю по лесу, дитя.
Летят вороны воровато,
Скрипят деревья недоверьем,
Кустарник сгорблен, как старик.
Как в паутину пауки,
Болото тянет две руки –
Меня в трясину унести.
И крик и карканье воронье,
А корни змеями шипят
Под непослушными ногами.
Поспешно убегаю вспять:
К маме, к маме, к маме.

РЫЖАЯ ДАМА

Юная рыжая дама по имени осень
Робко стучала рукою в перчатке златой.
Дверь отворил,
   и она заглянула мне в просинь
Глаз моих серых своею заветной мечтой.

И удалилась неспешно, степенно и важно —
Было напрасным занятьем её окликать.
В сердце, что билось тревожно, мятежно,
           отважно,
Хлынула зимнею стужей мирская тоска.

DREAMING

A child, I wander through the woods:
Like thievish crooks, rooks flying slyly;
Tree branches rustling in distrust;
A bush bent back like an old man.
Like spiders spinning stringy strands,
The swamp-mud stretches out its hands
To bog me down in miry lands.
The cackling caws of crows in summer,
Roots hissing like a snake in the rain...
With feet so heavy and benumbing,
I hurriedly run back again
To Mummy, Mummy, Mummy.

THE RED-HAIRED LADY

A young red-haired lady named Autumn — yes, Nature's
                                          own treasure,
Timidly knocked on my door with her gilded-gloved hand.
I opened the door,
        and her glance pierced my grey eyes' bright azure,
Eyes with her own cherished dream she so carefully scanned.

Then with slow steps she retreated in grandeur, unhurried,
'Twas useless to hail her, for we were now so far apart.
Just like a winter's frost, worldly angst flooded with fury
The trembling, rebellious, and once daring beats of my heart.

Translated from the Russian by John Woodsworth
5 April 2005
(Перевёл на английский Джон Вудсворт
5 апреля 2005 г.)

НАТЮРМОРТ

Мемориально на рояле
Роза алая стояла.
Роза алая стояла,
Высыхала, но не вяла...

Я увидел ликованье
Лепестков благоуханных –
В них застыло любованье
Мотыльковым трепетаньем.

ДОЧЕРИ

Пушистой лапкою котёнка
Душа смывает горечь слёз
При виде бедного ребёнка,
Что от меня вдали подрос...

Ты чистым васильковым взглядом
Высвечиваешь дно души,
И словно расцветают рядом –
Лесное чудо – ландыши.

Благоухая соучастьем,
В твоей душе живут цветы.
Ко мне тогда вернётся счастье,
Когда счастливой будешь ты.

STILL LIFE

In memory, upon a piano
In a vase a red rose rested
In a vase the red rose rested,
Faded but did not go flaccid.

I beheld a jubilation
In her fragrant, tender petals,
Frozen still in admiration
At the butterflies' vibration.

TO MY DAUGHTER

With a soft kitten's fluffy forepaws
I brush my sad tears off my heart
At seeing my poor heartfelt daughter,
Who's grown now after years apart...

Your azure eyes reveal the bottom
Of your pure soul, serene, profound.
As though there springtime lilies blossom —
A woodland wonder all around.

Your heart is filled with flowers as ever,
Diffusing fragrance to impart.
I will my happiness recover
When happiness attends your heart.

***

"Отчего ушёл?" – спросила.
И вопроса равной силы
Во Вселенной не звучало.
Его птицы прокричали,
Свои гнёзда покидая,
Листья скорбные в печали,
От берёзы отлетая,
И нахлынувшие тучи,
Прозвучавшие певуче,
Кучной влагой выпадая.
Отвечал до боли странно:
"Умирают люди рано,
Жизни смерть предпочитая,
И наносят сердцу рану,
Раной раны исцеляя".

***

Какая горькая истома
Им овладела ночью мглистой,
Когда ушёл от злого дома
Котёнок с лапкою пушистой?

И жизнь явила дно излома,
Луна закрылась тучей быстрой,
Когда ушёл один из дома
Котёнок с лапкою пушистой.

Не в сновидении, не в дрёме,
А чтоб оставить душу чистой,
Ушёл из гибельного дома
Котёнок с лапкою пушистой.

***
"Why'd he go?" she asked me coolly.
There was no greater question, truly,
Than that one in all creation.
All his birds in agitation,
Leaving leaves to mournful crying,
Left their nests in desperation,
From their black-white birch-trees flying.
Overcasting clouds had gathered,
Bringing on melodious weather,
Pouring water, deeply sighing.
I responded, strangely, surely:
"Humans die so prematurely;
All for death their life denying,
Giving hearts a wound so dourly,
Curing other wounds in dying."

Bitter Languish
***
What languish seized the fluffy kitten,
Upon a night, so gloomy, listless,
And made him leave the evil-smitten
Unfriendly home in the far distance?

The moon in clouds was quickly hidden
And life appeared a broken existence
When, all alone, the fluffy kitten
His home abandoned in the distance.

In neither sleep nor dream but bidden
To keep his soul clean in existence, –
So this was why the fluffy kitten
Left his doomed home without resistance.

***

Когда безмятежные йоги
Ступают по углям, как боги,
То им ничего,
У меня – возникают ожоги.
Когда безнадёжные снобы
Смакуют бесчувствие, чтобы
Скрыть чувство своё,
У меня возникают ознобы.

***

"Очисти дух, и взоры оживут", -
Так говорил в поэме Заратустра, -
Своей свободы пленники снуют,
В темнице духа суетно и пусто".

Явился Тот, кто взял грехи людей
И предложил последовать примеру.
Он призывал в душе своих друзей:
"В любви к последнему не знайте меры.

Что плоть моя, коль оставляю дух,
Очищенный от примеси лукавства?"
Огонь творенья в людях не потух,
Сжигает он холодное коварство.

***

When yogis walk barefoot so lightly,
Like gods, on hot coals glowing brightly,
They feel fairly good,
If I did that, I'd get burned forthrightly.
When snobs smack of being unfeeling,
Their own very feelings concealing,
So hopeless, they would,
I feel my whole body congealing.

***

"Cleanse the spirit and your eyes will awake"–
Thus spake Zarathustra in his lyric –
As freedom's own captives emptily ache
And fret in the prison of the spirit.

To take away sins from people Christ descends
And bids us follow His unique example;
Deep in his heart He calls upon his friends
To treat mankind with love, profuse and simple.

"What is my flesh to me now that I part
And leave my spirit unalloyed by evil?"
Creation's fire still burns in the human heart,
Consuming the cold and cunning wiles of the devil.

***

Я признаюсь, я – не охотник,
Что честолюбием томим,
Безмерной властью упиваясь,
Прицельным выстрелом лихим
Живую душу убивает.
А я настолько меланхолик,
Что даже и медвежья шкура,
Раскинутая вместо драпа,
Меня завидя, встанет хмуро
И в лес спешит закосолапить.

АНТОНИЙ И КЛЕОПАТРА

Портрет Антония не полн.
Светония Шекспир дополнил
Доподлино и в лицах:
Львицей Клеопатрой
Леопарда Рима – зримо.
Парад из града стрел
Страстей – и вдрызг сердца,
Но риск мерцать
Перед царицей
Агонии царей сильней.
Антоний к ней
Пучиной крови и безумств,
И муз,
Шальной стихиею Востока
Жестоко влеком,
Влеком и Стикса стоком.

***

Admittedly, I'm not a hunter
Obsessed by an ambitious goal,
And, so his boundless power enjoying,
With one quick shot a living soul
He kills so skilfully, destroying.
But I am such a melancholic
That even the bearskin spread before me
Across the floor in sullen slumber,
On seeing me, would rise, ignore me
And back into the forest lumber.

ANTONY AND CLEOPATRA

Antony's portrait's incomplete,
Suetonius' by Shakespeare enlarged
In characters large as life:
Through the Roman leopard's
Lioness, Cleopatra.
A parade of passion's hail
Of arrows – and hearts are crushed:
The rush to shine apart
Before the queen
Is stronger than the kings' agony.
And Antony,
Through the abyss of blood and mind-abuses
And muses,
Is driven wildly to her
By Oriental force, transfixed
As by the torrent of the Styx.

ГОЙЯ ГЕРЦОГИНЕ АЛЬБА

Я сам себя травлю нещадно ядом
Искусства, равнодушного к судьбе,
Я сам себя сжигаю взглядом ада,
Предчувствуя причастие к тебе.

Срываньем кожи сбрасыванье платья
Глубины обожания томит.
Правами ложа смерти и проклятья
Добыто обожение ланит.

ПОРТРЕТ ИНДИРЫ ГАНДИ

Она плывет богинею Лакшми –
Видением заоблачной горы –
Воздушной дымкой в белом сари
И, наполняя светом тонкий мир,
Народам драгоценные дары –
Наследие арийцев древних дарит.

***

Да, жизнь – растерянный калека,
Что просит милости у нас,
Проходит мимо человека,
Не подымая тусклых глаз.

Ее поэзия – колдунья
На помеле и знает ведь:
Душа-шалунья в полнолунье
Летит от нас на шабаш ведьм.

GOYA TO THE DUCHESS OF ALBA

I self-inflict art's poison with decision,
My art indifferent to my fate, I do.
I burn myself with art's infernal vision,
Anticipating I am part of you.

It tortures to the depths of adoration,
When you undress, it strips my skin, my breath.
Deification of your face in ardoration
Is won by rights of bedroom curse and death.

PORTRAIT OF INDIRA GANDHI

She sails like the goddess Lakshmi in the height,
Like a ghostly cloud-topped mountain range she drifts,
An airy smoke-cloud garbed in a white sari;
And filling the frail and delicate world with light
She gives away her dearly treasured gifts –
The precious legacy of ancient Aryans.

***

Yes, life is just a helpless cripple
With lowered dim, lacklustre, eyes,
Who, asking an alms from us poor people,
Ignores us all by passing by.

Her magic poetry bewitches
Just like a witch upon a broom –
Our prankish souls fly to the witches'
Sabbath at the full of the moon.

ВЛЮБЛЁННЫЙ ФОНАРЬ

Реку проходит вброд раскованно и смело
Сквозь утреннюю хмарь роскошная заря.
Ей лихо подмигнул: "Кому какое дело?"
От слякоти хмельной,
                    бесформенный фонарь.

Он плотно закусил куском сырого мрака
И делится теперь с веселою зарей...
Бродяги фонари, меж ними вышла драка –
Кто вспомнит о заре, тому и глаз долой.

***

Сердце шаманит ударами бубна,
Будит и манит волной состраданья,
Будто воистину благо доступно
При погружении в мир подсознанья.

Пусть, ударяя, безумствует бубен
В пляске шаманской – эмоции вихрем
Душу несут через сумерки буден
К новым скрижалям и праздничным играм.

ЕСЕНИНСКИЙ МОТИВ

"Не жалею, не зову, не плачу" –
Палачу плачу елеем сдачу:
Битым сердцем битвам песен,
Переписанным кульбитом.
Быта конь летит к орбитам,
Выбивая неба хруст
В розоватость утра уст.

THE LOVE-SICK STREET-LAMP

The rich, luxurious dawn with easy-daring brashness,
Crosses the river's ford in the foggy morning blush
A street-lamp winks at her: "Is it anybody's business?"
A dashing formless lamp,
                one slightly drunk with slush.

After taking a hearty bite of muggy gloom, so glum, then,
He shares it with the dawn so cheerful in the sky...
These street-lamps are just tramps; a fight takes place among them:
The one who remembers the dawn, away with his single eye!

***

Heart-pounding shaman's drum beats with exertion,
Waking, alluring with waves of compassion,
As if all good could be reached through immersion
Into a world of subconscious distraction.

Let that mad drum keep on pounding, so violent,
Dancing the shaman! The whirl of emotion
Carries my soul far away through days' twilight
Toward the new tablets, in festive commotion.

INSPIRED BY ESENIN

"No regret I feel, no pain, no sorrow"*
As I pay my doom with balm tomorrow,
Battle songs, with my heart beaten,
Like a somersault rewritten.
Life's horse gallops into orbit
Walloping the breaking sky;
Daybreak's rosy lips on high.

---

* First line from Peter Tempest's translation of Esenin's poem "No regret I feel..." (translator's note)

КРАСНОУРАЛЬСК

Труженикам тыла времён
Великой Отечественной войны

Красного уральского металла
С пламенным отливом – чистой меди –
Всей стране, как хлеба, не хватало
В годы разгоранья лютой смерти.

И с тех пор багряно-алым блеском,
Будто город меднокудрым стал,
Рдеют городские перелески
Листьями, впитавшими металл.

НАЗАРЕТ

На заре Назарет взором неба объят.
Тайны неба хранят неоттаянный взгляд,
Ветер севера веером веет,
Лето клевером сумерки стелет,
Алым маком горят ореолы лучей,
В спор вступил с синевой к воле склонный
                                ручей.
Склоны гор на заре цвета спелых гранат,
Кроны яблонь
            кроят свой восточный наряд.
На полях тени гор, что с угрозой заре,
Закрывают собой от небес Назарет.
Вифлеемской звездой залетел в Назарет,
Синеву разорвав, огнедышащий свет.

KRASNOURALSK

*To those who toiled on the home front
during the Great Patriotic War*[*]

Pure cast Ural copper, sanguine-red –
Our whole nation was as direly hungry
For this fiery metal as for bread
When death flamed ferocious through the country.

Ever since with crimson scarlet lustre –
Just like curly locks turned copper-hued! –
City groves are gleaming with bright clusters
Of red leaves, with metal now imbued.

NAZARETH

Nazareth is embraced by the afterlight skies.
Heaven's secrets disguise their unthawed, calloused eyes;
While the winnowing wind wafts a north cold;
Summer's clover-like twilight unfolds;
When the poppy-red sunset bursts over the hill,
Streams then challenge 'the blue' to a test of sheer
                                                                         will.
Hillsides filled with ripe pomegranate afterlight;
Apple trees by their side
                        flash their Eastern gowns bright.
Hill shadows in the field, while a threat to the sky,
Shade the whole of Nazareth from the heavens on high.
Like the Bethlehem star, tearing through the blue night,
Into Nazareth's sky flew a fire-breathing light.

---

[*] *Second World War*

ГОРЕ

Согласно Гегелю, у горя
Внутри свечение другое:
Как молчаливость при укоре.
Как реагировать на горе?
Как на предгорье,
Когда подняться надо в гору.

СУД

Суд Ореста, Сократа, Иисуса...
Кто из нас избежал суда?
Видно смысл слов души "Вознесусь я" –
"Я возницей несусь сюда".

Жрицы храма суда суровы,
Судный день – очищенье души,
Изваяние чувства нового:
Не покаешься – согрешишь.

Умывание рук – омовение:
Мысль, познавшая лишь себя, -
Обретающая обновление,
Отрезвляемая судьба.

За пределы сознания выйти
И осмыслить его как предел –
Всё равно что из ямы вырытой
Для себя сотворить надел.

SORROW

As Hegel holds, inside of sorrow
There is a different light to borrow:
Keep silent when reproached tomorrow.
How should you treat befalling sorrow?
Just like the hollow
As up the mount you have to follow.

JUDGEMENT

Judged are Orestes, Socrates, Jesus...
Who of us escaped judgement severe?
'I'll ascend' read His soul's words – but this is
'I'll descend in a chariot back here.'

Judgement priestesses – harsh in their temple;
Judgement Day – to cleanse souls from within.
The new model of feeling is simple:
If you do not repent, you will sin.

Now a washing of hands is Ablution:
Thought that knows its whole self in full view
Is a fate sobered up from illusion,
An existence conceived, born anew.

Stepping out of the box of cognition
Seeing thought as a limit itself
Is like finding a fresh excavation
And then digging a grave for yourself.

РАЗДУМЬЕ

На заброшенной Земле
Увядает простота,
Только голос аппаратов
Все становится сильней,
Он привычно вызывает
В человеке суету
И лишает между делом
Сокровенного пути.
Если только человек
Не услышит зова дали,
Суета и празднословье
Не дадут устроить рая
На растерянной Земле.

***

Памяти Л.Н. Мартынова

О понимании творения в стихах
Стихали звуки строк, что приходили,
Но прихождением оставили возможность
Забыться, то есть стать за бытием.
Что говорило бытие в забытых строках,
Смогу ли это я воистину узнать? –
Да, если овладею этостью и узнаванием.
Они способны мне придать могучесть
Проникнуть в смысл строк,
                         которые забыты –
Живут не только лишь за бытом,
Но за пределом бытия.
У этих строк могуча их живучесть,
Она ответствовать способна тайно
Вопросу о природе бытия.

MEDITATION

On the poor, neglected Earth
Simple measures fade away.
Only voices of machines
Grow still louder day by day,
While habitually spreading
Vanity through all mankind,
And depriving, at odd moments,
Humans of their sacred path.
If these human beings heed not
Cries of help from far away,
All their fuss and empty words
Won't establish Paradise
On a squandered, wasted Earth.

***

In Memory of L.N. Martynov

The sounds of the lines that came have died away —
The lines that told of versified creation
But once they came they could no longer be
Forgotten, i.e., begotten be-yond being.
What being was saying in begotten lines forgotten —
Is that a fact that I can ever know?
Yes, if I possess concreteness and enquiry.
By them I am empowered and entitled
To penetrate the sense
            of lines so long forgotten —
That live, have being, not only just for getting
But getting be-yond the boundaries of our seeing.
These lines have life empowered by their vital
Ability to respond — respond in secret —
To the question of the nature of all being.

*(Co-translation by Ivan Zhavoronkov and
John Woodsworth)* (*Совместный перевод
Ивана Жаворонкова и Джона Вудсворта*)

РОЖДЕНИЕ ФИЛОСОФИИ ИЗ ДУХА ПОЭЗИИ*

Миф, эпос, логос –
    и в эйдос голос воплощён.
Вопль ещё не слышен, но совет нехилой
    схолией даёт Эсхил:
"Плач сотворите, но благо да верх
    одержит!"
Бхага обернулся благом пред
    становленьем Богом.
Влагой слёз слез с небес Дионис и донёс
    благую весть,
Её влагая морфием в арфу Орфея.
У феи-мистики неистовая мысль
    бытийствует анимистичностью,
Но это алетою в поэзии снялось,
    добавив света.
Газели рифм Гомера и Сапфо
Глазели нимфами из тьмы души поэзой
    света в лету.
Мистерии сокрыли сакральную историю
    мышления.
Мысль тлением хранит, а не хоронит
В Хроносе, пламенный язык,
Что ведал огненность архэ поэмой
    Гераклита.

---

* Эйдос – идея, вид, образ; схолии – объяснения, поясняющие примечания к какому-нибудь тексту; логос – слово, смысл, закон бытия; Бхага – божество, даритель обильного богатства; архэ – первоначало мира и познания; алета (алетейя) – несокрытость, неутаённость бытия.

THE BIRTH OF PHILOSOPHY
FROM THE SPIRIT OF POETRY*

Myth, epos, logos —
                and voice was conferred on the *Eidos*.
The noise of crying yet unheard, *Æschylus* gives us advice
                in a solid scholium,
"Create a cry, but the good will still come out
                on high!"
And Bhaga turned to good
                before becoming God.
In the sweat of tears Dionysus came tearing down
                from the skies, the good news to advertise,
Its wet morphia mist morphing into Orpheus' harp.
While the mystic fairy's daring art
                animexisted in the animistic.
But this met with elimination in verse by the *aletheia*
                which added illumination.
The gazelles of Homer's and Sappho's rhymes
Gazed, like nymphs, out of the soul's dark blight,
                like the poesy of light in *lethe*.
Mysteries would have secreted
                the sacral history of thinking.
Thought bears it alive – not buries it
In Chronos as a flaming arching tongue that knew
Through Heraclitus' verse
                the ardour of the *arche*.

---

* *Eidos – idea, vision, image; scholium – an explanatory note or comment on a text; logos – word, thought, the law of being; Bhaga – a deity, a god of abundant wealth; arche – the first principle of the world and knowledge; aletheia – the disclosedness, unconcealedness of being.*

У подлинности бытия возник язык.
Кинь зов в архэ – возникнет эхо,
Возницей прилетит и вестью об алете
                                      вознесётся.
Милетцы, мысли первые атлеты,
Талант дерзания атлантами держали:
Дразня поэтов, пролетели Лету.
Поэтому Сократ наметил эйдосу
                                      нетленный путь идеи
С критикой на демос, и Демокрит его
                                      приветил.
Потом Платон в тон платы за Сократа
                                      сакральным стал апологетом.
Пал в эйдос голос, и логос
                                колосом пророс.

From the genuineness of being sprang the genesis of language.*
Give hail to the *arche*, and it will echo,
Come flying, like a chariot, regaling with
                the cheerful tidings of the *aletheia*.
The Milesians, the first great athletes of thought,
Fought like Atlases to balance the talent of daring,
Sparing the poets no mercy, flaring their way past the Lethe.
This is why Socrates guided the *Eidos*
                in the undecaying way of *idea*,
To question the place of the *demos* and Democrites
                          embraced it.
Then Plato, plainly to pay back for Socrates,
          played the role of a sacral apologist.
Voice fell to the *Eidos* to call us
            and the *Logos* rose as a colossus.

(*Co-translation by Ivan Zhavoronkov and
                      John Woodsworth*)
(*Совместный перевод Ивана Жаворонкова
                и Джона Вудсворта*)

---

* That is, philosophers began to speak truly about being.

ПУЛЬС МИРА

Слышишь вампира шагов
Тихий стон за стеной,
Леденящие душу шелесты?
Это дыхание першингов
Стужей сковало стальной
Земные немые челюсти.

Шеренги першенгов иглами
Гибельными воткнуты в сердце
Живое родной Земли.
Отгородившийся виллами
Америки, Англии, Греции
Растущему пульсу внемли!

***

Сердце Бетховеном слышит Германия,
Гойей прозревшая видит Испания,
Видит Италия всполохи смерти
Ликом мадонны и римской керамикой,
Требует смерти крылатой изгнания
Голос страдания – реквием Верди.

***

Германия, ответь своей поэмой,
Чеканным ритмом, Гёте языком,
Какое из мгновений пропустить,
Остановить какое нужно время.
Прекрасное мгновение бегом
Промчится, невниманья не простит.

THE PULSE OF THE WORLD

Do you hear the steps of the vampire
Softly groan o'er the wall,
And the rustles give sighs, heart-congealing?
This is the Pershings' respiring,
Whose iron-like ice-frost has stalled
The earth's jaws benumbed and unfeeling.

The Pershings in ranks are stationed
Like death-bearing spears that pierce
Our Earth's living heart, dear and weak.
Give heed to the growing pulsation —
You who are fenced in by villas
American, English and Greek!

***

Beethoven's heartbeats are heard in Germania;
Goya's broad canvasses waken Hispania;
Italy views the rebirth of the vanished
Through the Madonna's face, Roman ceramics;
Verdi's own requiem, the voice of great panic,
Claims that the black-wingèd death should be banished.

***

O Germany, respond with your own poem,
With measured rhythm, Goethe's lyric tongue,
Pray tell which of the moments to neglect,
Which of the periods should be stopped from going.
A moment of sheer beauty on the run
Will not forgive a simple lapse unchecked.

Так всё же быть или не быть,
Любить иль не любить? Что скажет
Англия? Великого вопроса
Шекспировского ей не позабыть.
А разве Гамлет королей указам
Безумие не предпочёл, а росы

Кладбища всем винам во дворце?
Ему дворцы явили сверхбезумие,
Смертельное для искренней души,
Хранившей память об отце...
А ныне будь, страна, в раздумье
И Гамлетом смысл жизни поищи!

Идёт борьба за право для планеты
Быть в солнечной семье – девятой,
За пробужденье разума от сна.
Что сделал бы с крылатою ракетой
Тот, кто и в мельнице крылатой
Врага в своём отечестве узнал?

Какой сократовский вопрос
Ты, Греция, ещё не разрешила
О смысле жизни и добра,
Что человек в веках пронёс,
Познав себя, набравшись силы,
Свет мироздания вобрав?

"To be or not to be?" still asks mankind,
To love or not to love? What says, in sadness,
England? This greatest of Shakespeare's questions
It will not ever put out of its mind.
Did Hamlet not prefer accepting madness
To serving the kings' orders and suggestions,

The graveyard dew — to all the wines of the court?
The sovereign courts had caused his brain's frustration,
Destroyed his heart that kept, sincere and kind,
His father's memory alive, in thought...
All people, give yourself to meditation,
Life's purpose now through Hamlet seek and find!

Our planet's fighting for the right as yet
To be a ninth kin member of the sun,
To wake its mind from sleep, so deep, profound.
And what would he who even saw a threat
In a winged windmill to his land have done
With a winged missile*, were he now around?

What question Socrates engages
That you, Greece, to resolve is not empowered,
On the meaning of good and life,
That man has carried through the ages ,
And known himself, accruing power,
Absorbing all creation's light?

---

* Or: 'armed windmill' and 'armed missile' (translator's note)

Афины помнят след Сократа:
Не только ног его босых,
Но губ его на чаше с ядом,
Напоминающий стократно
Целебность жалящей осы,
Летающей над тучным стадом.

А цель сократовских укусов –
Прославить мудрость человека,
Не очернив его души,
Не изменив природе вкусов...
И Диоген был стойким греком,
Но в бочке с порохом не жил.

Верленовской томительной печалью,
Отчаянностью юного Рембо,
Виолончельным чаяньем Вийона
Взволнованная Франция встречала,
Как "лезвие под левое ребро",
Военную программу Пентагона.

А чёрный дым над Нагасаки,
Что укрывает Белый дом,
В нём прибавляет белых дум?
Слезит глаза горелый факел?
Палёный воздух ловят ртом?
В ушах стоит преступный шум?

Athens remembers Socrates' trace:
Not only his bare feet but, yes, the clasp
Of lips upon his cup of poison,
Reminding us in a hundred ways
Of healing help from stinging wasp
Now circling o'er the herd so noisy.

The aim of Socrates' stings:
To praise man's wisdom and acumen,
Without the blackening of his soul,
True to his tastes and other things...
Diogenes – a stalwart human –
No powder-keg in his home's hole.

Through the tormenting sadness of Verlaine,
Through the sad despair of young Rimbaud,
Through the cello-like yearnings of Villon,
All France was vexed now to accept with pain,
Like "a knife stuck into the ribs too low,"
The war-plan project of the Pentagon.

Black smoke from Nagasaki's slaughter,
Dimming the White House fine and fair,
Paints all its black thoughts white for years?
The burnt-out torch makes their eyes water?
They gasp for breath of hot burnt air?
The vicious blast rings in their ears?

***

Отдалённый дым, даримый,
Все народы мира знают:
В этот мир Лонгфелло входит,
Трубку мира с белым дымом,
Что до неба, предлагает
Неустанно всем народам.

Белый дым к созвездью Лиры
В поднебесье устремился,
Струны Лиры, словно арфа,
Заиграли гимны мира,
Звонкий звук засеребрился
Вегою – звездою альфой.

Свет звезды дорогу кажет
Путникам, во тьме идущим,
Кораблям в далёком море,
Ангелам небесным даже,
Ну а миру – долю лучшую,
Избавление от горя.

***

All mankind in this creation
Knows the smoke that has been gifted:
Into this world Longfellow enters,
Gives the peace pipe to all nations,
Tirelessly, with white smoke drifting
High toward the heavens' centre.

To the Lyra constellation
White smoke raced through space so lightly;
From Lyre's harp-like chords are pouring
All the anthems of the nations,
Silver sounds resounding brightly,
Through Star Alpha, Vega, soaring.

Light the shining Star has given
Wayfarers on path benighted,
Distant ships until the morrow
And celestial angels even,
To the world the best share's plighted –
Full deliverance from sorrow.

Parthenos by Elena Makarova

ZARATHUSTRA

A lyrical philosophical poem
inspired by F. Nietzsche's
Thus Spake Zarathustra

ЗАРАТУСТРА

(по мотивам произведения
Ф. Ницше
„Так говорил Заратустра")
Философская поэма.

Санкт-Петербург
1993

*Посвящается памяти поэта
Леонида Николаевича Мартынова*

ЗАРАТУСТРА В ДОЛИНЕ

Горят у зари уста, остыв, острыми
Глазами в озеро уставленной.
С восходом узорной зари сходит с горы
Заратустра к холодному озеру,
Десятилетье назад оставленному.
Видит — роща слепа, слышит — ропщет тропа:
Мол, без слуха и духа его с той поры
У стихов и духов беспризорность тропы,
Выпадает строфа и строка не строга,
И мгла, как игла, прилегла в приозёрность.
А соль слезает с лица от солнца слезой,
Вестью лестною чествуя счастье светила.
Плавить злато в устах Заратустра устал,
Встав от сна, предстает златоустом сутра:
«Чтобы сталось, светило, со счастьем твоим,
Если б ты никому никогда не светило?
Стало б льстиво частями себя мне,
Если б вместе нам не творить у стиха рост,
Небелый и белый стихи сочетая
Сплавом из гордости — мудрости тающим?
Я орлом гор достиг, змеёй думы растил
Из мёда и яда туманной мудрости
И с вестью к людям иду я по совести,
Свет и весть не сведя воедино в себе.

*Dedicated to the memory of the poet
Leonid Nikolayevich Martynov*

ZARATHUSTRA IN THE VALLEY

The illustrious star arises; the dawn's sharp eyes
Staring at the lake and her lips aglow.
As the morning dawn ascends, down the mountain descends
Zarathustra towards the cold lake in the valley
That he had to abandon ten long years ago.
He sees the sightless trees, he hears the trail bewailing
That, no sound of his spirit resounding since that time,
The untrod trail of spirit and verse is in decline;
The stanza strikes out and the strophe is not strict,
And gloom, like a harpoon, looms piercing the pondside.
Yet a salty solar tear slides down his face,
Humouring that orb's euphoria with toadying tidings.
From mouth-melting gold Zarathustra felt tired and old;
Golden-horned after sleep, he beholds the morn,
"Your euphoria, Orb, it would not be absorbed and gone
If your orbit never shone for anyone?"
Would you spread for me your parts in a flattering way
If the two of us did not increase our verse,
Blank and unblank lines in time combining
In melting mix of high-flying pride and wise?
I pried from an eagle's high and a serpent's lie
From honey hocks and toxins of misty wit;
Now I, clear-conscienced, bring people the tidings,
The worldtide and the tidings untied inside me.

Белой льдины таянием тянут меня к вам
Рифы моря – морфием рифмования,
Рифмомания, мифов мир духа моля,
Крылатыми нимфами манит к стихам.
Людей одаривать жаром од иду я,
Самых мудрейших радуя глупостью их,
Самых беднейших – богатствами тихими.
Благославлю тебя, спокойное светило,
Коль можешь ты без зависти светить мне
Как величайшему в блаженстве человеку.
В мир выплёскиваю я себя из чаши
Сияния храма твоего блаженства.
Я, преисполненный золота жаром,
Спешу к вам алою коровою зари,
Струящей розовое молоко – рассвет
Лёгким облаком небесного пожара».

***

Так мыслями отчаянно сгорая,
Тропой с горы спускался Заратустра.
Зашёл он в перелесок незаметно,
А мыслями на мысы выплывал,
И старца пред долиной повстречал.
Тот хижину священную оставил
Корениев нетленных поискать.
Когда был взором пойман Заратустра,
Кореньев собиранье прерывая,
Он в корень мысли зренье устремил:
«Я узнаю тебя, о Заратустра,
Мне памятны твои глаза-костры,
Паденьем звезд метающие искры.

Like a snow-white melting iceberg I'm drawn to you
By seas' lime reefs and rifts of shifting rhyme,
With rhythm's pleas to the spirit's world of myths,
As I'm made to drift to verse by wingèd nymphs.
I've come and have bestowed the warmth of odes
To tantalise the wisest with their folly,
The poorest to surprise with quiet wealth.
I'll bless you, star serene, in all your glory,
If you, unenvied, will but shine for me —
For one who has the greatest bliss on earth.
Into the world I pour myself from the cup
Of the radiant temple of your heavenly bliss.
Brimming over with the heat of molten gold,
I hasten to you as to the scarlet cow of dawn
Streaming with rosy milk — the light of a newborn day —
Descending through wispy clouds of heavenly fire."

***

Thus scorched with thoughts and with despair afflicted,
By mountain path descended Zarathustra;
Unwittingly he wandered into woodlands.
But drifting up to promontories in thought,
He met an elder at a valley plot.
That old one had just left his holy cabin
In search of undecaying, unrotten roots.
When with his eyes he captured Zarathustra,
Breaking his seeking, he picked up a thought,
And fixed his eyes upon the root thereof,
"I recognize you well, O Zarathustra;
Your eyes the bonfires I remember by
Their shooting fiery sparks that star-like fly.

Ты из долины нёс на гору прах свой,
А ныне ты огонь несёшь в долину.
Скажи, ужели не боишься кары,
Которой люди наказуют за поджоги?
Твои глаза ясны, как у ребёнка,
Гребёнки вместо можно было б ими
Причёсывать лохмотия души
Людей, непробуждённых ото сна.
Их не буди, им этого не надо.
Твоей наградой за стремление
Дать людям много счастья будет смерть,
И впредь тебя врагом сочтут за это.
Нельзя любить их и не умереть.
И оттого от них я удалился,
Что больше своей жизни их любил.
Теперь моя любовь лишь только к Богу.
Ты много счастья людям не давай,
Чтоб не считали скаредой и вором.
Ты бедным людям милостыню кинь
И вскоре уходи, чтобы не сгинуть,
Гниенья их досыта надышавшись».
Так говорил святой и мудрый старец,
Поникшею походкой удаляясь,
И песен окруженье, словно свита
Земных богов, с ним вместе уплывала.
И вслед ему подумал Заратустра:
«Однако я не настолько беден,
Чтоб людям только милостыню дать.
А бедный старец, видимо, не знает –
В лесу в глуши и вести не дано –
О том, что Бог уже не умирает,
О том, что боги умерли давно».

You carried then your ashes to the mountain,
You carry now your fire into the valley.
Pray tell, do you not fear to be chastised
Unkindly as an arsonist by humankind?
Your very eyes are pure like those of children;
They could serve as a comb in rearranging
The shuffled and dishevelled locks of souls
Of people unawakened from their sleep.
Do not awaken them, they do not want it.
For your reward for trying to give people
Too much of happiness will be but death,
For that you will be deemed a foe thereafter.
One simply cannot love them and not die.
And so I found myself from them withdrawing
Because I loved mankind more than my life.
And now my love alone to God is tendered.
Do not give people too much happiness
Lest they should think you niggardly and thieving.
Just throw the poor some alms and get you hence
As quickly as you can, lest in departing,
You breathe too much their stinky rotten odour."
Thus spoke the saint, an elder man of wisdom
As he with lagging footsteps then retreated;
With songs surrounding him just like an escort
Of earthly gods now floating off with him.
And in the elder's wake thought Zarathustra,
"However, I am not so destitute and needy
To give the people paltry alms alone.
In these back woods no herald has been crying,
The poor old man does not quite seem to know
That God in heaven is no longer dying.
But gods upon the earth died long ago."

***

Так забрёл Заратустра в город в предгорье,
Скучая, на рынке толпился народ.
Канатный плясун, что был отроду в горе,
Толпе показал свой на землю полет.
Толпа посмеялась разбитому оземь:
Он ей показался ничтожнее всех.
Звенели слова, Заратустра их бросил:
«Сомнение вызвала жизнь человека –
Обязанный быть обезьяной навеки,
Он грязи потоком предстал и изъяна.
Откуда вычерпывать море для чистки
Его, обречённого скоро погибнуть?
Канатом над бездной лежит человек,
Исчезнуть легко человеку в той бездне.
Благое течение жизни зову я
Презрением, вызвавшим миг омерзенья.
Призвание ваше высокое в жизни
Откинуто горькими думами века.
Люблю я стремящихся к гибели в бездну –
Сгорают они от обители сердца.
Люблю человека за это паденье,
В котором от мрака его избавленье.
Моя добродетель – стремленье к паденью,
В нем искры борьбы с человеческой тенью».

***

Расплавленной лавой вулкана словá
Его разливались, стекая рекой
В холодное озеро кормом для рыб.

***

Zarathustra the path to a foothills town followed,
The market place crowd dully swarming around.
A sad tightrope dancer who'd all his life sorrowed
Performed for the crowd, soaring down to the ground.
And he, shattered to earth, was amid the crowd's laughter;
He appeared to them to be the most worthless of all.
There resounded these words — Zarathustra had dropped them,
"The life of mankind raises doubts of a kind;
For man that is meant to be monkey forever
Has turned into a mud stream and flawed imperfection.
What part of the sea should one possibly draw from
To cleanse humankind, that is doomed to soon perish?
Just like a tight-rope mankind is stretched
Across an abyss, and could easily vanish.
I call the good course of existence contempt, for
It causes within me a feeling disgusting.
Your lofty vocation in life is refuted
By bitter and centuries-ageing reflections.
I love those aspiring to die in the deepness —
They burn from the hearths of their hearts, in consumption.
I love them for falling in deep desolation;
Where from deepness of gloom one can find one's salvation.
My virtue is striving for such degradation
Showing sparks of the strife with mankind's adumbration."

***

Just like a volcano's molten lava, his words
Overflowed in eruption, flowing down as a river
Straight into a cold lake, as feed for the fish.

А люди ушли с головою в себя,
В молчании рыбою стали опять,
Морганием был их ответ на слова,
И пылью рассыпались пёстрой они.
И вот Заратустра остался один,
Он в сердце устало подумал, любя:

***

«Сегодня был для них совсем немного я
Глупее местных откровенных дураков.
А им для счастия всегда недоставало
Любую мудрость просто глупостью назвать.
И оказали мне доверие трупа
Последнего из тех и жалких и презренных,
Которые опасностью для жизни злой
Лишь снова жизнь свою стремятся обеспечить,
Но тем уже над бездной смерти поднимаясь.
Улов сегодня – ни одной живой души
И тело мёртвое впридачу получил.
Ты будь спокоен, мой достойный мёртвый друг,
Душа твоя была томительно бедна,
Она плыла мертвее доблестного тела,
Разбитого совсем предательством души.
Намерен сам тебя похоронить, как ты
Стремительно хоронишь душу в тело».

***

Тропа трепала путника, устало
Труп спутника взвалившего на спину.

But people went deep into themselves, apart;
And fish they became in the silence again,
In response to his words, they blinked for their part;
And scattered, dispersing, like the motley dust blown.
And here Zarathustra was left all alone;
He lovingly, wearily mused in his heart:

***

"Today I looked to them only a little more foolish
Than any frank, outspoken local fool.
It would have always added to their happiness
To call any wisdom nothing but simple folly.
So I have been entrusted with the corpse,
Of the last of the pitiful and despisèd—
Who vigorously strive once more to regain life
Endangering, though, their wicked life's existence
But thus now rising over death's abyss.
Today my catch is not a living soul
And I've gained a dead body in the bargain.
Never you mind, you worthy dead friend of mine,
Your soul was miserably, lingeringly, poor,
It seemed to float more dead than your noble body
Broken apart by your own disloyal soul.
I intend myself to bury you as is your goal
To bury your soul within your own dead body."

***

The trail wore out the weary wayfarer treading
Along, with his companion's body on his shoulders.

Могильщики при встрече с Заратустрой
«Собакой дохлой» труп его назвали,
Советую скорей оставить город:
Мол, нынче шло ему одно везенье,
Раз он, как чёрт, прилип к собаке дохлой
И тем себя унизил добровольно;
Поэтому его и не убили,
Но дней его листанье прекратится,
Когда презрение к нему исчезнет.
И так усмешкой гримируя лица,
Жрецы могил перекосились на него.
Спокойно миновал их Заратустра,
Движенье с телом к лесу продолжая.
Чередованье дней перебирая
Срединой сердца об усердии людей,
Он думал: «Убиение меня
Они считают легче убиенья
Той вечности, что их до их рожденья
Убила властию страстей убогих».
Увидев дом, он стал стучаться в двери,
Пока себя не обнаружил голос
Восставшего от сна с постели старика.
«Кто в сон идёт?», – спросил. – «Живой и мёртвый.
Жилище дайте нам, питье и пищу.
Голодного случайного кормленье
Есть насыщение собственной души».
Старик исчез, потом вернулся снова,
Вино и хлеб поставил перед гостем:
«Голодность мест пригодна к поселению.
А почему не хочет есть твой спутник?» –
Спросил старик. Ответил Заратустра:
«Уговорить его мне будет трудно,
Чтоб ел он также, как и я. Он умер».

The grave gravediggers meeting Zarathustra
Remarked the corpse was a dead dog he carried,
Advising him to leave the town, and quickly.
They said that it was fortunate that he
Had stuck to that dead dog just like the devil,
So of his own free will himself he humbled.
That's why he wasn't slain but spared the killing.
But his life's leaves will cease to turn in places
Whenever his humiliation ceases.
Their sneering masks concealing their grave faces,
The grave-yard priests then looked at him askance.
But Zarathustra passed them by, so tranquil,
On to the forest with the body of his neighbour;
Retracing in his heart of hearts the labour
Of people through the cycle of their days
He deeply thought, "They count it easier
To murder me than those eternal moments
Which killed them long before their birthed existence,
By their poor passions strongly overpowering."
On seeing a house, he knocked upon the door
Until the voice of an elderly man awakened
From sleep, barely out of bed, made itself heard.
"Who comes into my sleep?"—"Both dead and living.
Give food and drink to us, give board and lodging;
One's opportunity to feed the hungry
Is one's fortuity to refresh one's soul."
The elderly man withdrew but then returnèd
And put down bread and wine before his caller.
"The hungry place is good for habitation.
But why will your companion not eat also?"
The old man asked, and Zarathustra answered,
"I hardly shall be able to persuade him
To eat the same way I do. He is dead now."

«Кто он? Мне это всё равно. Имею
Один для всех закон гостеприимства.
Пусть он съедает поданное мною».
Продолжив путь тропою, Заратустра
О трудностях питания размышлял:
«Голодные места для поселенья
Избрал старик лишь для того, чтоб скрыть
Смущение своё за ту Вселенную,
Которую он выбрал для рожденья,
И оттого, кроме Вселенной, нечем
Пленённых ею путников кормить».
В лес дальше углубился Заратустра,
Нашёл огромное дупло в деревьях,
Вложил туда неспешно свою ношу,
Из чрева дерева могилу создавая.
Потом заснул и вновь проснулся свежим,
Себя он обновлённым обнаружил,
Взор, брошенный на понятую Землю,
Искристой истиною новой засветил:
«Теперь нужны мне спутники живые,
Они б могли пойти за мною сами,
А мёртвым это всё-таки труднее:
Натаскивая, их приходится таскать».

***

Листья роняет холодная осень,
Стылую почву чуть грея собой.
Слёзное листьев падение оземь
Выплачет чистого неба покой.
Истину новую с новой скрижалью
Сердцу сказал он златыми устами:

"Who is he? Well, I do not care. I have but
One law of hospitality for all.
Let him consume what I have kindly offered."
Continuing on his pathway, Zarathustra
Reflected on the challenges of food,
"The hungry places fit for habitation
The elderly man had chosen for himself
To hide his self-disgrace over the Cosmos
Which he himself had chosen as his birthplace.
That's why imprisoned wayfarers are nourished
By nothing but the Universe itself."
And on into the forest plunged Zarathustra
And found in there a hollow tree, enormous;
Unhurriedly he placed therein his burden,
The huge tree's womb into a tomb converting;
Then fell asleep and soon awoke refreshened,
And found himself anew rejuvenated.
He cast a glance upon the Earth well-known,
His eyes agleam anew with sparkling truth,
"I need companions now, not dead but living,
Who would themselves be able me to follow;
For, after all, it's harder with the dead ones:
One has to train and trail them along behind."

***

Autumn makes forests let fall their own leafage,
Keeping the earth slightly warm with the sky.
Tearfully will keep on falling their foliage
Till the serene heavens weep themselves dry.
Truth, born anew, from a newly-born tablet
Golden-tongued he to his dear heart was saying,

«Нечего с речью мне впредь обращаться
К старым и мёртвым угасшим мечтам.
Надо мне на дом не более двух
В слух обращённых отшельников тонкий.
Счастьем своим освещу их сердца,
Песни мои откровеньем исполнятся:
Гордость и мудрость — орёл и змея,
Солнце спокойно им светит, смеясь».

"Never again will I speak to my daydreams,
Ageing and dead ones and withered away.
Truly indeed, I now need at my home
Two homely hermits with delicate hearing.
I shall illumine their hearts with my bliss,
Songs will pour forth from me through revelation.
Serpent and eagle are wisdom and pride;
Sunshine enfolds them with calm, smiling light."

РЕЧИ ЗАРАТУСТРЫ

Тонким слухом ставшим скажу я о духе —
Роль его занятна ему и для слуха.
Он сначала вроде породы верблюда
Может вдруг заставить своё неразумье
В тон светиться грёзами в духе довольном,
И получит способность смеяться он
Над собой и старыми звёздами всуе,
Благо, внутри не спешит измениться.
Вдруг вызван не страх, а враждебность к науке:
Львом становится дух, меняя испуг на
Дерзость, смело ставшую умной и доброй,
Слово «должен» на слово «хочу» меняет.
Где возьмёт он слово «лечу»? Это слово —
Речь ребёнка и произнесть его просто:
Дух — ребёнок новый творит мир свободно
Там, где лев расчистил верблюжьи сказанья.

**

Воздух застенчиво-чистый в горах.
Духи со звоном в лучистых крылах
Между вершин пролетают в снегах.
Гордый, опасный и радостный дух
Мой возвышением чудно парит.
Вы с вожделеньем глядите на верх;
Вниз, оттого что возвышен, смотрю.

ZARATHUSTRA'S SPEECHES

To the finely tuned ears will I speak of the spirit —
His own role is of interest to him, those who hear it.
In the begging beginning his nature, a camel's,
Can of a sudden compel his un-wisdom
To illumine with daydreams in satisfied spirit,
And he will become capable of laughing now
At himself and the old constellations in vain;
Good he's in no rush for changes internal.
Inspired not by fear but by hatred of science:
A lion the spirit becomes and his fear is
Replaced by audacity, kindly and clever;
'I will' is now for 'You shall' substituted.
From where does he gather the words "I am soaring"? —
These words are but childish and to say them is easy:
Spirit—the child now creates a new world in freedom
Where Lion has now brushed away Camel's stories.

***

Timidly pure is the air in the mounts;
Spirits with wings iridescent with sounds,
Midst snow-white pinnacles flying around.
Proud is my spirit, and dangerous, glad,
Soaring in splendour on heavenly heights.
Up do you longingly look, as for me,
Down do I gaze—for exalted am I.

Смелым, способным насильем крушить
Видеть приходит нас мудрость души.
Вы говорите, мол, трудность есть жизнь, —
Нежность к себе покрывает обман.
Розе труднее, чем вам, выносить
Капли трепещущих свежестью рос.
Лучше пред жизнею не трепетать.
Любите вы не привычкою жить,
А привыканьем к любви, что болит;
Дух неумело в ней каплей сокрыт.
В росах бутона горячечных роз
Стынет любовию сон в лепестках,
Счастье осмысленное – в мотыльках.
Слёзы блаженства сверкают в глазах
При наблюдении маленьких душ.
Демон серьёзности губит и вас,
Но не прогонит его голый гнев,
Только отклонит бессонницы смех.

***

Стремишься ты к величию в вышину,
Душа твоя взывает к звёздам духа,
И дурь твоя к свободе устремилась,
Уставясь ввысь, как дикая собака,
Что гавкает из конуры сердито,
Луну облаивая в тишине.
Живут такие пленники свободы,
И мудрость их становится лукавой.
В темнице духа сыро и темно.
Очисти дух, и взоры оживут,
Светить начнут любовью и надеждой,

Brave and coercive destroyers to come—
Such would the wise soul want us to become.
You say that life is a difficult thing,
This is your tenderness covering your lie.
Harder it is for the rose to endure
Fresh, trembling droplets of morningtide dew
You'd better not tremble before life itself.
You love to live life not by habit but by
Getting accustomed to love — and that hurts,
Hiding a droplet of Spirit, inexpert.
Dew-pearled, upon rosebud petals ablaze,
Sleep glazed with love, resting peacefully, lies;
Happiness known is within butterflies.
Teardrops of blessedness gleam in my eyes
Seeing them, observing them, these little souls.
The demon of seriousness slays you as well;
Over it barren wrath will not hold sway;
Sleeplessness' laughter will turn it away.

**

You so aspire to an exalted height,
Your soul is craving for the stars of spirit;
Your foolishness has also rushed for freedom
Just like a wild dog staring up to heaven
And barking angrily out of the doghouse,
Baying the moon upon a tranquil night.
There dwell on earth such prisoners of freedom
That their sagacious wisdom turns deceitful.
The prison of the spirit – damp and dark.
Cleanse the spirit and your eyes will awake
And will at once with love and hope illumine,

Иначе будет ваше возвышенье
Способно к низости и благородству.
Опасность не в добре, а в разрушеньи
Его святыни личностью твоею.
Язвительностью гибельного яда
Она способна рушить высоту
Свободного парения блаженства.

***

Есть на свете проповедники смерти,
Им по виду неприметному верьте.
Встретим их мы легендарным поверьем:
Наша жизнь, мол, продолжается благом
После смерти, — утешению рады.
Этой сказкой постепенно их надо,
Лишних, из жизни выманивать тихо.
У них нет выбора, кроме терзанья
Страстью этой — умереть, лишь родившись,
И смеются той соломинке жизни,
Скажу я вам, что страданием держит.
Они от того мгновения в страхе
Перед жутким вырыванием жизни.
Миг страшит самим отсутствием смерти.

***

Сильней всего страшишься ты, что будут
Тебя щадить ничтожные зануды:
Ведь нам всего страшнее милость к нам.
Я не щажу не терпящих пощады,
Чтоб не упились низостью своею.

Else your own elevation be disposèd
Aspiring toward both nobleness and meanness.
The danger's not in good but in destroying
Its sacred sanctuary by your nature.
By viciousness of a pernicious poison
Your nature can destroy the lofty height
On which the blissful blessedness soars freely.

***

There are preachers of death in all places:
You discern them by their unassuming faces.
Let us welcome them with the conviction
That our life will continue existing
After death — for our own reassurance.
From this life, one by one, one must lure them,
The superfluous ones, with this story.
They have no choice but self-laceration
Directly they're born, with a death-wish.
And they mock the last straw of existence—
I will tell you—it holds them by suffering.
They are frantic with terror at the moment
Their existence is ghastly uprooted.
It's the absence of death that's most frightening.

***

You dread the most that you be given mercy
And spared by petty bores who render pity:
For mercy is to us what we dread most.
I do not spare him who despises sparing
Lest he should revel in his sordid meanness.

Награда — побежденье человека.
Врагами вы презренных не имейте,
Себя не унижайте мелким другом.
Когда вы бессердечны, я люблю
Сердечности взаимную стыдливость.
Когда в себе уродливо мерзки вы,
Имейте мужество, чтоб не стесняться.

***

Смотрите на больных горячкой обезьян,
Стремящихся к вершине власти и
Так дурно пахнущих от несварения
При жадном поедании друг друга,
Начавших службу новым их богам:
Назвали воровство образованием,
Газетой — изрыганье горькой желчи,
服忍ением — извращение души.
Спешу рекою сомы горечь од вам
Направить, чтоб втекала в кровь, пьяня.

***

Стремлением к истине вы называете страстность,
Стремлением к сущему я назову вашу боль.
Хотите вы сущее мыслимым сделать? — Давайте,
Покорным оно быть должно отражением в духе.
Мудрейшие, это стремление к власти всецело,
Оценки торжественной волей зовутся у вас.
Пускаете вы по реке бытия свою волю.

The true reward is when mankind's surpassèd
Those whom you loathe do not consider foes.
Do not demean yourself with petty friends.
At times when you are heartless, then I love
Our mutual chagrin at souls kind-hearted.
When you within are loathsome, mean and ugly
Take manly courage not to be embarrassed.

***

Just see the feverishly sick, too eager apes
Striving to reach the very heights of power,
And smelling foully bad from indigestion,
While avidly devouring one another,
And worshipping their idols newly made:
Referring to common theft as education,
'Newspaper' means the vomiting of black bile,
'Church service' is their term for soul perversion.
I push the gall of odes as a soma river
To flow into your blood and make you drunk.

***

'Pursuit of truth' you call impetuous passion,
'Pursuit of being' is what I call your pain.
Do you want to make being conceivable? — Go to, then,
It should be a meek reflection in the spirit.
O wise ones, this is naught but a lust for power;
Estimations of value you term 'triumphant will,'
And add your own will to the river-flow of being.

***

В руки убийцы беги из мечты
Женщины страстной, иначе – погиб.
Духом рождается горе из грязи:
Не дай к себе прикоснуться тому,
Что целомудрием все называли.
Вместо кровавого красного мяса
Просит оно подаянье у духа.
Дьявол, что изгнан, в свинью перешёл:
Ты не гони, чтоб свиньёю не стать.
Вместо него поселяется глупость,
Мы к ней не шли, но она к нам пришла.
Женщина скрыла раба и тирана,
В ней сочетается светлое с тёмным,
Но и в мужчине полно нищеты.
Ты не ищи в них достойного друга,
Друга создай из себя самого.

***

Шум великих тебя оглушает,
Жало мелких уколет осой.
Где начнётся твоё одичанье,
Там холодного плена покой.
Студнем стынут все соки у сердца,
Его раны нальются свинцом.
Дирижирует демон оркестром
С перекошенным страхом лицом.
Люди будут хвалить его игры
В жизнь и смерть, только ты не играй,
Уходи в своё личное эго,
Постоянно в себя убегай.

***

Flee from the dream into the murderer's hands;
Dream of a woman of passion and you're dead.
Sorrow is born as pure spirit from filth:
Do not in any way let what is called
By everyone virtuous chastity touch you.
Instead of the red bloody meat it is begging
Sorely for merciful alms from the spirit.
Into the swine went the devil cast out:
Cast it not out lest you turn into swine.
Instead of the devil there comes to dwell folly,
We did not go to it but it came to us.
Woman conceals both the slave and the tyrant,
Brightness and darkness together inside her;
Yet inside the man, too, is fullness of want.
Do not seek in them a friend trustworthy;
But be a loyal friend unto yourself.

***

You are dazed by the noise of the greatest,
You'll be stung by the wasp of the small.
Where your wildness will take its beginning,
There you're caught in cold rest once for all.
Heart's blood freezes in stiff congelation;
And its wounds will be filled up with lead;
While a devil conducts the orchestration,
With his face seized with terror and dread.
They will praise him as he keeps on playing at
Life and death, only you should not play;
Just delve deep down within your own ego;
Ever into yourself run away.

ЗАРАТУСТРА В ГОРОДЕ

Пошёл по шёлку неба Заратустра, небо
Через живую ширму облаков смотрелось
Улыбкой мокрой со слезами в мостовую.
Его калеки обступили ульем пчёл
В надежде мысли разобрать аукционом.
Один из них, горбатый с виду, обратился:
«Как водопад в горах шумит, взметая брызги,
Так в имени твоём роится мысли буря,
Алмазные пылинки слов разносит в души,
Воспламеняет их гореньем чистой мысли,
И люди, словно звери водопоя, жаждут
Послушать речи, обречённые на благо.
Тебя за бога почитать всегда мы будем,
Коль нас, убогих, исцелишь телесно чудом».
Им Заратустра отвечает исцеленьем:
«Смотри, слепой, на мир — его глубины видишь
Срединой сердца, мир прекрасным созерцая.
В счастливом пребываешь состояньи грёз.
А если зренье дам, увидишь мерзость жизни
И в скорбь великого страдания душа
Твоя впадёт, немилосердно изнывая,
И станешь ты отчаянно несчастным в мире.
Смотри, горбун, на то, какую роль благую
Всю жизнь играет несравненный гордый горб твой.

ZARATHUSTRA IN TOWN

Upon the silken skyway set out Zarathustra,
The heavens through the living cloth of clouds appearing
Smiling through tears down at the bridge across a highway.
The cripples then surrounded him like a hive,
In hopes of getting his ideas by auction.
And one of them, a hunchback, started speaking,
"As noisy waterfalls send splashes in the mountains,
A whirlwind storm of thought within your name so rages,
Spreading the diamond dust of words upon our souls
Igniting them with the fire of pure thought,
And people, much like beasts at waterholes, thirst
To hear the speeches destined for the good.
We shall give honour to you as a god forever
If only by a miracle you'll heal our bodies."
And Zarathustra did respond with healing,
"Behold, O blind, the world — you see its deepness
Within your heart of hearts, beholding the world's beauty.
So happy you are, being in a state of dreams.
But if I give you eyes, then you shall see life's meanness
And in the sorrow of great suffering, your soul
Will fall with wailing inconsolable,
And on earth you'll become despairingly unhappy.
Look, hunchback, what a good hunch it has been playing,
That proud, incomparable hunch in your existence:

Благодаря ему ты научился чуять
Все чаянья людей к себе и к миру, ум твой
Развился в звонком чувстве. Ты ж, негодный,
Желаешь уничтожить благодетеля».
Горбун в смятении: «Да, верно говоришь ты,
Но почему сказал всё это столь открыто?
Своих иначе учишь ты учеников». —
«С горбатым говорю я выпуклою речью».

***

Дарит Заратустра с выходом из города
«Пёстрая корова» новое сознание:
«Золота предназначение высокое,
Это бескорыстия светятся ценности.
Кроток и блестящ взор у добродетельного,
Высший бескорыстный жертвенный дарящего
Взгляд, и у него дарить себя желание.
Ваша цель — остаться жертвенными самыми,
Надо вам богатства в духе скопить тайного.
Вещи привлекайте все к себе насилием,
Чтоб текли обратно вновь дарами вашими.
Станет любовь грабить ваши драгоценности,
Этот назовёте миг своекорыстием.
Так его святым сочтёте мигом светлого.»

***

Вечно бедный голодный другой эгоизм
Алчно бродит, подобно собаке больной,
Голод вечен его, неуёмен в душе,
Ужас нашего чувства ему говорит:
Вверх идёт и наш путь к роду сверхчеловека.
Дух у тела товарищ в борьбе и победе.

Thanks to your hunch, you've learnt to sense all expectations
And people's hopes for you and the world, your mind
Developed in sound feeling. But you good-for-nothing,
You want to do away with your good-doer now."
The hunchback in dismay, "Yes, you did say this truly.
But why in the world did you say that all so bluntly?
You teach your own disciples something else."—
"I speak with hunchbacks in a bunched-up way."

***

Zarathustra gives us, while leaving the city
Called "The Motley Cow," a brand new consciousness:
"Gold's predestination — to be much more valuable;
So brightly beam the values of unselfishness.
Meek and illustrious the soft glance of the virtuous;
Supreme, sacrificial, unselfish the bestowing one's
Glance; to give of himself he has a readiness.
Your goal is to remain yourselves a sacrifice;
Secret riches of the spirit to accumulate
And draw all things toward yourselves coercively
So they'll flow once again as your gift-offerings.
Should your love start stealing all your precious jewelry,
You shall give this moment but the name of selfishness.
And call it a moment of holiest enlightenment.

***

Yet another selfishness, ever hungry and poor
Like a sick dog, rapaciously prowls all around;
Unappeasable as ever — its hunger at heart;
And our terrified feeling would speak to it this:
Our upward course, too, rises toward supergenius.
The spirit supports the body in struggle and conquest.

Если сердце подобно потоку у вас —
Дух разбужен от сна, благородный, восстал.
Если сердце, подобно потоку, бурлит,
Служит благом и страхом своим берегам, —
Ваша воля нашла полюбившее сердце,
Мыслью стала и раннею мудростью духа.
Тайны взмахов крылатого завтра
Носят тонкому слуху упрямую весть:
Новым сияньем приходит сверхчеловек».

**

Сказал Заратустра, а после добавил:
«Как лев на охоту выходит неспешно,
Орёл поднебесьем плывёт в вышине,
Иду так один без попутчиков дальше.
И вы в одиночестве путь продолжайте,
Себя защищайте вы от Заратустры —
Быть может он вас обманул, обольщая.
Врагов всех не только любить вы учитесь,
Своих же друзей ненавидеть умейте.
Венок мой лавровый вы рвите усердно,
Иначе почтенье ко мне вас раздавит,
Коль статуей рухнет, разбившись в осколки.
Себя обретайте, теряя меня вы.
Послушайте притчу мою на прощанье:

**

Спал Заратустра утром голодный,
Тихо к нему подползала змея.
Сонно лицо прикрывал он ладонью,
Когда укусила ехидна, смеясь.

If your heart among others resembles a stream,
Then your noble spirit wakes to rise from sleep.
If your heart, like a river, one day overflows,
Both a blessing and a curse to its lowland banks,
Then your will has discovered the heart of a lover,
Early wisdom of spirit and thought — has acquired.
Now the secretive wing-beats of the stealthy morrow
Send to delicate ears the persistent good news:
As the supergenius with a brand new radiance comes."

***

So said Zarathustra, and after that added,
"As a lion unhurriedly walks out for hunting,
As an eagle through heaven sails high in the sky
So I keep on going without my companions.
You also your way on your own should continue,
And guard yourselves, too, against Zarathustra,
For he may as well have deceived you alluring.
Do not learn to love all your enemies only,
But learn how to hate all your friends and acquaintances.
Tug hard at my laurel wreath and pull it with vigour;
Your reverence for me will otherwise crush you,
Decomposing to smithereens, just like a statue.
And do find yourselves each time I am abandoned;
Give ear to my parable now in our parting:

***

Now Zarathustra slept hungry one morning,
A snake slithered stealthily right to his side.
As he covered his face with his hand in the dawning,
The viper quite suddenly bit him and smiled.

В глаза заглянул той змее Заратустра —
Смутились ехиднины злые глаза.
«Спасибо тебе: разбудила под утро», —
Так он змее добродушно сказал.
И добавил: «Прими благодарность,
Скоро я отправляюсь в свой путь».
А змея отвечает в тональность:
«Чтобы ноги в пути протянуть». —
«Разве страшен мне яд, для дракона,
Яд обычной гремучей змеи?
Не лишайся его, дорогого,
Для себя и для бедной Земли».
И ехидна накинулась снова
Возвратить драгоценный свой яд,
И она оказалась готова
Снова рану его зализать».

Deep into the adder's eyes gazed Zarathustra;
The serpent's confusion shown in treacherous eyes.
'I thank you for waking me up in the morning' —
He said to the serpent in a kindly tone.
He then added, 'Accept my thanks truly.
I shall soon now set out on my way.'
But the serpent in kind then retorted:
'To turn up your own toes on the way!' —
'How could I as a dragon be frightened
By the poison of a commonplace snake?
Do not waste it, your own precious poison,
For yourself and the poor Earth's own sake.'
And the snake lunged again, not to kill him
But to take back her poison, impugned.
She turned out to appear to be willing
To restore him by licking his wound."

ВОЗВРАЩЕНИЕ ЗАРАТУСТРЫ

Речи посеяны в почву пашни души,
Всходят словами как семя проросшее.
В замке пещер Заратустра отдых нашёл.
Много идей созревает в думах его
И прорастанием больно давит своим.
Смысл созревает и тянет жаждой дарить,
Злаки в стремлении к людям рады расти,
И проросла изобильно мудрость его.
Боль и страдание мысли семя дают,
Скорой свободой и пламя дышит ещё.
В сон Заратустры приходит вещий старик
С зеркалом, с озера гладью схожим во тьме,
И говорит: «Посмотрись, узнай ты себя».
Ужас объял Заратустру — видит: не он —
Смотрит надменно упорно демон, шутя.
«Что означает знамение? — думает он, —
Видно значенье его — искажение
Нового данного мною учения.
Видно назвать захотели сами себя
Плевелы, жницы боясь. Назвались они
Гордо пшеницей, другое имя приняв.
Враг исказил Заратустру в вашей душе,
И потому я теряю дружбу людей».
И Заратустра вскочил, сияя лицом:
«Счастье-безумье моё оставлю себе,
И позволяет оно друзьям передать:

ZARATHUSTRA'S RETURN

Parables sown in the soul's own arable soil
Sprout forth with words, just like seeds, germinating.
As Zarathustra finds rest in castle-like caves,
Many ideas ripen among his own thoughts
Pressing him painfully, sprouting forth with all force.
Meaning ripens, too, and impels giving by thirst.
The corn is glad to increase in number for men,
And his own wisdom has grown abundantly so.
Anguish and suffering pain give seed to thought;
The flame breathes more and more with forthcoming freedom.
In Zarathustra's sleep comes an old seer-man
Bringing a smooth lake-surfaced mirror in the dark,
Saying, "Look, and you will recognize yourself."
Horror seizes Zarathustra — he sees not himself
But the devil staring back at him, mocking with jest.
He wonders "What can the vision possibly mean?"
The deduction is this: a serious corruption
Of what I have said in my latest instruction.
Evidently the tares, fearful of being pulled up,
Wanted to proudly call themselves wheat,
Hoping to be spared by taking a different name.
Foes have deformed Zarathustra now in your hearts.
That's why I'm losing my friends among humankind."
And Zarathustra leapt up, his face now agleam,
"I'll hold on for a while to my mad-happy joy.
It allows me to address my friends in this way:

Стал я устами ручья, дающего жизнь,
Мой поток ринется новым руслом реки,
Он пробивает дорогу в сердце людей.
Как созидающий, старым жить я устал,
Дух не желает истоптанных башмаков.
Чтобы ускорить своё сказание, я
Прыгнул в мятежную бурю, радость даря,
И в колеснице хлестаю диких коней.
С речью к кому обращён, того и люблю.
От напряжения тучей грозной грозя,
Льюсь благодарною речью в ваши умы.
Дикая мудрость моя дитя принесла.
Люди, готовьте ему приюты в сердцах».

***

А берёзовая роща стоит:
Соблазняет золотом малахит,
Обольщает зеленью желтизна
И тоскует проседью белизна.
Скоморохом мох, развалясь, лежит,
Мухомором вздох на груди ожил.
Паутины тень налегла в грибах,
Гильотиной день у зари в губах.

***

Северный ветер сыплет смоквы с дерев.
Вверенным словом станет мудрость моя,
Спелыми сок и мякоть слова летят,
Мир примиряет ладонями полдня
Сонную осень землистого неба
С томным ненастьем влюблённого моря.

I've become now the mouth of a life-giving stream;
My waters rush forth in a new river-course,
Breaking its way into people's own hearts.
As a creator I'm tired of living by the old;
My spirit no longer wants old, worn-out shoes.
Rushing to make my own speech run faster, I
Joyfully leap into hurricane's eye,
Spur on my chariot, whip the wild steeds.
Those to whom I address my words I love.
Filled with the tension of violent thunderous clouds,
I pour myself into your mind, giving thanks.
Wild wisdom within me has brought forth a child:
People, make room now for him in your hearts."

***

And the birch grove stands a wonder, behold:
Its green malachite seduces with its gold;
And its yellow leafage tempts us with its green;
And its whiteness wholly misses its grey sheen.
Like a skomorokh lies the moss beneath —
Like a toadstool heaves its breath to breathe.
Mushrooms eclipsed by the shadow of a web;
Daylight cut off by the sunlight lips' ebb.

***

Blowing north wind shakes the figs from the trees.
A trustworthy word my wisdom will be.
Sweet falls the juice, and meat of the word.
Peace is now made with noon's hands between heaven,
Drowsy and earthy, in autumnal slumber,
And a love-languishing sea's abominable weather.

Избавьте себя вы от горя-страданья
Блаженными радостями созиданья.
Чувство томится пленённым в темнице,
Молот оно в разбивании камня.
Образов образ чувство видит в себе,
Светом приходит к людям сверхчеловек!

***

Блаженны поэты, что ищут блаженных
И нищих мечтами холёных бабёнок
И пишут стихи им о море и моле,
Морочат измором их дух во плоти.
В отстойной канаве пристойность картины
Тушуется рябью, мол, так — глубока.
Но разве не море — павлин из павлинов,
Хвостом распластавшись, снуёт в берега?
Распущенно разно, красуется праздно:
Ему всё равно перед кем красоваться,
Хотя б пред коровой, которой под кровлю
Иль просто на луг поскорее забраться.
Морока, умора: от этого моря
Стремятся быстрее подальше убраться.
Несите мечты на вершину повыше,
Сожгите их все постепенно смелее,
Их пепел предайте стихии из сини.
Люблю я стихийное море, сердито
Со мною поспорить готовое жарко.
В нём вечность, влекущая женщиной скрытной.

From suffering, sorrow, find your liberation
In blissful elation of joyful creation.
Feelings incarcerated suffer in prison,
They'll be the hammer the hard stone to shatter.
An image of images feelings see in themselves:
The *overman* comes to the people as light!

***

How blessed the poets that seek blessed women,
So meagre in dreaming, soignée, soft of skin, and
Compose for them poems on sea and seacoast,
Deceiving their spirit, consuming their flesh.
In storm-sewer ditches the scene of decorum
Is stirred up by ripples, suggesting some depth.
And is not the sea a true peacock of peacocks
With tail spread awry, sweeping over the sand?
Its tail is spread widely, displaying itself idly:
Who the onlookers are, it cares not to ponder,
Maybe even a cow chewing cud in her cowshed
Or starting across her lush meadows to wander.
This sea's such a nuisance, a terrible bother,
That they're hastening to quickly betake themselves yonder.
Go carry your daydreams high up to the mountain
And bravely ignite them one after another,
Disperse then their ashes through the azure-blue heaven.
I love it, this sea elemental and angry
So ready for heated dispute, as it harbours
The secretive woman's eternal attraction.

***

Интригует на рассвете синева,
Сочетает необычные слова:
Распластало покрывалом листопад,
Акробатом станет ветер выступать,
Дирижирует оркестром лунный свет,
Дипломирован маэстро — сам медведь,
Декларирует повеса соловей,
Демонстрирует завесу суховей,
Заклубил клубнику пеленой туман,
Пригубил рассвета пламени обман,
Выпивает залпом у росы красу,
Уплывая, лапой роется в лесу.

***

Лужайка, окаймлённая кустами,
Бежала родником среди поляны
Лесных хмельных цветов и пьяных трав.
Газелями с косулями игриво
Кружили её душу в танце девы.
«Танцуйте впредь, — сказал им Заратустра, —
Противник духа тяжести отныне я,
Спою для танца вместо Купидона:
В твои недавно заглянул я очи,
И жизнь казалась мне непостижимой».
Мне жизнь насмешкой лёгкой отвечала:
«Изменчива и женщина во всём я,
Притом не добродетельна и дика.
Назвали вы меня глубокой тайной,
Одаривая, как и все мужчины,
Своею добродетелью меня вы».

***

At dawn one is amazed by the heavenly blue,
Marrying unordinary words on cue:
Like a comforter the leaves cover the ground;
Like an acrobat the wind performs its round;
The moonlight conducts the orchestra fair;
The graduate maestro is actually a bear,
Wild oats are sown by the nightingale;
While the dry wind rustles the night-time veil;
The fog has o'er the strawberries a blanket now o'erstrewn,
Tasting the illusion of the new dawn's fiery plume,
Draining all the beauty from the dew for good,
Floats away, its paw still digging in the wood.

***

The little green meadow flanked by Nature's bushes
Wound through the glade, just like a little river,
Midst drunken grass and tipsy forest flowers.
Just like gazelles and roes, the playful maidens
Spun giddily like the drunk soul of the meadow.
"Dance from now on," said Zarathustra to them.
"Henceforth I am against the spirit of heaviness,
And will sing to your dance instead of Cupid:
I looked, O life, into your own eyes lately,
You seemed to be unfathomable to me."
And life replied to me with light derision,
"I'm changeable in every way, a woman,
And — what is more — I'm wild and void of virtue.
You've always referred to me as a deep, dark mystery,
And, as is every man's prevailing custom,
You have endowed me with your own good virtue."

Смеялась так она невероятно.
Но я не верю, если говорят о
Самой себе столь дурно и с досады.
«Смотрите, — залетела мудрость, тая, —
Ты любишь жизнь, поэтому и хвалишь».
Ответить злобно мне ей захотелось,
Сказать всю правду мудрости сурово:
«Люблю я жизнь, её же ненавидя,
На нашу жизнь похожа мудрость наша,
Поэтому я к ней привязан так же».
Спросила жизнь: «А что такое мудрость?». —
«Её сетями ловишь — ускользает,
Изменчива, кусает часто губы,
Фальшивой предстаёт прекрасной дамой».
Смеялась жизнь ответу Заратустры:
«Быть может обо мне вновь говоришь ты?
Тогда скажи о мудрости, что знаешь!»
Раскрыла жизнь глаза возлюбленные,
Казалось погружаюсь в них я снова.

***

Ночью душа моя — бьющий родник,
Очень спешит она влиться в парник
Песен, могущих лететь напрямик.
Жажда любви моей хочет сказать:
Света сосцами упьюсь наповал.
Если бы только я тёмным бывал,
Звёздочки, вас бы благословлял.
Собственный свет меня пламенем жжёт:
Мне не знакомо то счастье даров,
Света чужого я зреть не привык.

She laughed so that one hardly would believe her.
And I do not believe her when she speaks so
Ill of herself and out of deep annoyance.
"Look here," said flighty wisdom, quickly melting,
"You love life — and on that account you praise it."
I wanted to reply to her with anger,
And speak the entire truth to wisdom harshly.
"I love life, yet hate it even as I love it;
Our life and wisdom bear such strong resemblance
That I feel attached to life in any case."
Life asked me: "Just who or what is this wisdom?" —
"You try to catch her, but she's much too elusive;
She's fickle, and lip-biting's her incessant habit,
Deceptively posing as a beautiful lady."
But life only laughed at Zarathustra's answer,
"Perhaps it is me that you are once more describing?
So tell me whatever you know about wisdom!"
Life opened wide her own deep eyes beloved;
While into their pupils I sank down more deeply.

***

Nightly my soul gushes up like a fount,
Rushing to merge with the heat of my round
Of songs that shoot straight to the heart and astound.
Thirsty, my love is now longing to speak:
Sucking the breasts of light ever so hard,
I'd give almost anything to be wholly dark,
Then I could bless you, my dear little stars.
Scorched by the flames of my own dazzling light,
I have not experienced the gladness of gifts,
I'm not used to seeing a light besides mine.

Не отдыхает от яркой ночи
Зависть моя: солнца вижу глаза.
О, пресыщение дара души, —
Горе дарящих всех — голода сыть.
Голод растёт моей льющей красой:
Мной одарённых ограбить бы мне.
Месть измышляя так, злобно дарю
Нежность с тревогою, льющею яд.

***

Туда, к могилам юности моей
Несу вечнозелёной жизни цвет
К виденьям юности моей любви.
Вы умерли, видения мои,
Теперь струите сердца сладкий яд.
Богатый самый одинокий я —
Цветущий для воспоминания
Возлюбленных и добродетельных.
Подобием пугливых птиц пришли
К желанию моему доверчиво,
Попали дикой злобы стрелы в вас
И поразили птиц моих надежд.
Проклятье против вас, мои враги:
На кратное разбили вечность вы,
Напали призраками на меня.
Когда-то моя юность говорила,
Что дни её священны быть должны.

***

Насмешливым чудовищем таятся
Скептические призраки души,
Возвышенностью духа тяготятся.
Охотничей добычи не ищи.

Bright is the night, and my envy does not
Rest from it now that I see the sun's eyes.
O satiation with gifts from my heart —
A surfeit of hunger — the givers' own woe.
Streaming with beauty, my hunger now grows:
Those I have gifted I wish I could rob.
Plotting my vengeance, I spitefully give
Tenderness streaming with poisonous angst.

***

Down yonder to the tombstones of my youth
I carry a bloom of everlasting life,
Toward the visions of the youth of my love.
I know you visions of mine are already dead.
Now stream with your sweet poison to my heart.
I am the richest and the loneliest one—
I, flowering now in loving memory
Of my own virtuous and beloved ones.
Just like a flock of timid birds, you came
Once to my eager longing, trustingly.
The arrows of wild malice struck you hard,
Killing the birds of my own cherished hopes.
The curse against you all, my enemies:
You've taken my eternity apart;
And just like phantoms, you've assaulted me.
Long time ago my youth used to consider
That holy ought to be all of her days.

***

They hide, like scornful monsters, in derision
The sceptic apparitions of the soul
That crave the spirit's lofty sublimation.
To seek the hunter's spoil is not your goal.

Из познанного леса возвращался
Высокий дух, сражавшийся с зверьми,
Выглядывал он диким и кусался —
Сам тигром стал, играющим с людьми.
Высоких дум не трогайте величья,
Они величием утомлены
И, скидывая бременем обличье,
Нагими в духе предстают они.
Томленьем наступает свежий день,
Себя в себе снимает дух и вьётся,
Прыжком преодолеет свою тень —
Получит шанс на попаданье в солнце.

***

Смеяться должно мне от страха пестроты,
Увидев родину горшков и красок всех:
Десятками цветов обмазанные лица
Сидели к удивленью — настоящими.
Вокруг вас множество зеркал, польстивших вам.
Поистине вам масок лучших не найти —
Подобье лиц есть подлинные лица,
Народы из-под них выглядывают пёстро
Религиями, нравами, мечтами.
Подёнщиков в подземном мире тени
Полнее и жирнее вас, живущих,
Скорее их бы предпочёл, чем вас, живых.
Действительность способна вызывать лишь
Залётных птиц сплошное содроганье.
Гордитесь настоящестью своею,
Всецелостью отсутствия поверий,
Хотя совсем ещё гордиться нечем.
Картины вы тому, чему поверья ваши.
Действительность погибели достойна.

Returning from the forest of cognition,
A lofty spirit fought with beasts unkind
Gazed out untamed and biting, in addition
Became a tiger playful with mankind.
Let it alone, great thinkers' sublimation,
Of their sublimeness they are tired withal;
When casting off the weight of self-deception,
Naked of spirit they show themselves to all.
In anxious anguish a new day begins,
The spirit now casts off itself in whirling;
If he his shadow overleaps in spins,
He'll have a chance to strike the sun in twirling.

***

I had to laugh at my fear of the diverse,
On seeing the mother of all pots and paints:
The faces dyed, with dozens of bright colours,
They sat there looking surprisingly present-day.
There are many mirrors 'round that flattered you.
Indeed, you could not possibly find better masks —
The likenesses of faces are true faces;
From out these masks all peoples peep diversely,
With their own dreams and customs and religions.
The underworld day-laborers residing
In shadows — fatter and fuller than you living —
I'd rather have them than all of you who live.
All that reality is capable of doing
Is to make birds of passage shake all over.
You seem to take great pride in your existence,
With utter absence of beliefs entirely,
Even though you still have nothing to be proud of.
You are but pictures of your own perceptions.
Reality as is deserves to perish.

***

Луна собралась солнце породить в рассвет,
Она лежала тяжкой и широкой, в болях,
В своей беременности лгуния-луна.
Я больше верю человеку на Луне,
Чем лучшей женщине — женьшеню исцеленья.
Ночной с нечистой совестью мечтатель,
Конечно, и с мужчиной схож он мало:
Котом на крыше сторонится окон,
Проходит звёздными коврами в ночь он.
Мужские ноги, поступью негромкой
Подобные луне, крадущейся в ночи,
Своею лживостью не знают уваженья.
Сравнение даю всем познающим чисто:
В любви их стыд и совестью нечисты.
Похожи на луну все любящие землю,
Назвать вас надо похотливыми лжецами:
Презрением к земному полон дух ваш,
Сильней его все внутренности ваши.
Вещает дух вам ваш: «Без вожделения
Смотрю на мир, а не голодною собакой,
Счастливым в созерцаньи с мёртвой волей
Луной-глазами осязаю землю.
Моё познание вещей пребудет чистым,
Подобно зеркалу лежать пред ними буду».
Невинности недостаёт в желаньи вашем,
Поэтому порочите желанья.
Чувствительные лицемеры, похотливцы,
Божественные шкуры прикрывали
Кишенье змей с их запахом дурным.
Сперва осмельтесь вы надёжно верить
Себе самим и внутренностям вашим.

***

The moon got ready to bear a sun into daylight;
She lay so broad and heavy, in her birth-throes,
In her own pregnancy, the lying moon.
I would sooner believe there is man on the moon
Than the best ginseng woman as the woo-man's cure.
With all too bad a conscience the night-dreamer –
Indeed, with man he has little common meaning –
Like a cat on a roof he slinks by all the windows
And over night-time starry carpets limbers.
The feet of men that tread so softly, gently,
Just like the moon that steals along by night,
Earn no respect from their dishonesty.
I put this parable before all pure discerners:
Their love holds shame, their conscience much impureness.
For all earth-lovers bear the moon resemblance,
You should be designated lustful liars:
Your spirit holds the earthly in derision,
Your bowels, though, are stronger than your spirit.
Your soothsaying spirit tells you: "Without desire
I look upon the world, not like a dog a-craving;
With deadened will yet still a happy conscience,
Through moon-like eyes the Earth I am perceiving.
Henceforth I shall perceive all things with pureness,
I will prostrate myself before them as a mirror."
Your innocence of desire is insufficient,
And therefore you defile all your desiring.
You sensual hypocrites, voluptuous and lustful,
Your god-like skin exterior has enshrouded
A teeming swarm of snakes with their bad smell.
You first must dare to believe yourselves intently,
Your inward selves, indeed your very bowels.

Вздымается желанье богом жажды,
Из глубины морей восходит жадно ввысь,
Оно желает целования солнца.
Подобно солнцу, жизнь люблю и глубину.

      ***

Горы рогами коров врезались в брови туч;
Капает алая кровь — сгусток зари тягуч.
Остров распластан китом, фонтаном кита — вулкан,
Острой простудой дыша, — бешеный великан.
Палуба кружит народ, видит народ полёт:
Прямо летит тень в вулкан, в сторону не свернёт,
Тень Заратустры вплыла в недра Земли средь дня.
Люди спросили о нём: «Видимо, чёрт унёс?» —
«Нет, — раздавалось в ответ. — Видно, он чёрта взял».

      ***

Туча — у сумерек шаль,
Облако — солнца вуаль,
Радуга — неба корсет.
Молами языка
Берег прибой лакал
С пеной и зубьями скал.
Море стонало в ответ
Криками чаек чуть свет.

Desire, the god of thirst, divinely rises,
Ascending thirstily from sea depths into heights;
It would be kissed by sunshine with hot passion.
Just like the sun, I love life and all its depths.

***

Just like cows' horns, the mountain-tops pierce the dark clouds' brows:
Red blood is dripping in drops – thickened by the sunset's bows.
The whale-like isle lies flat; its volcano a volatile spout;
Breathing with a cold sore throat – a volatile giant throughout!
The tossing ship gives a bad fright as people behold the flight:
The shadow flies straight for the crater, no shadow of turning aside —
Zarathustra's floated inside the Earth's bowels in broad daylight.
People then wondered of him: "Looks like the devil took him."
"No!" the reply really shook — "Looks like the devil he took."

***

Dark clouds are twilight's dull shawl;
Bright clouds are sunshine's bright veil;
Rainbows are the girdle of the sky.
With the tongues of the moles,
The breakers lapped at the shoals,
With the teeth of cliffs in foamy rolls.
Sea billows moaned in reply,
As seagulls at dawn gave their cry.

ТИХИЙ ЧАС

Что случилось, что случилось, что случилось?
Я опять спешу покинуть вас внезапно,
Но медведь не хочет лезть в свою берлогу,
Вас оставить силы нет у духа-страха.
Кто зовёт меня, какой тревожный гений?
Это он — суровый бог моих мгновений —
«Тихий час» зовётся в мире тонком, сонном.
Он со мною в вечер тихо спорил скромно,
И ушла из-под меня, страдая, почва.
Сон степенно взял к себе, благословляя,
Испугалось сердце тишины покоя.
«Тихий час» безмолвно молвил еле слышно:
«Ты прекрасно знаешь это, Заратустра,
Но не смеешь молвить сам себе от страха,
И не хочешь сам себе признаться, слабый».
И заплакал как ребёнок я невольно:
«Это свыше моих сил и не могу я?».
Голос вновь ответил: «Что тебе за дело
До всего до этого, своё скажи ты
Откровенье и разбейся». Я ответил:
«Жду я более достойного». Но слышу:
«Нет тебе ещё пока благословения». —
«У подножия своей вершины стоя,
Я живу, ещё никто не смел сказать мне
То, что ты», — заплакал я в ответ негромко, —
И хотя я к людям шёл, но мимо плыли
Речи и не доходили до сознанья». —

THE QUIET HOUR

What has happened? What has happened? What has happened?
I rush again to leave you of a sudden,
But to go back to its lair the bear's unwilling;
The spirit-fear has no strength to forsake you.
What frightening genius calls upon me?
This is he — the stern, ingenious god of all my moments, —
Called 'The Quiet Hour' in the world, exquisite, sleepy.
At evening he argued with me in shy silence:
The suffering ground gave way and sank beneath me.
Sleep soon overtook me, blessing me serenely;
And my heart got frightened by the quiet stillness.
Barely audibly the Quiet Hour spoke then, voiceless,
"Full well you know it, don't you, Zarathustra,
But you don't dare say it to yourself, you're fearful,
And will not admit it to yourself, you're feeble."
Against my will I cried out like a baby:
"It's beyond my strength and I can't really do it?"
But the voice replied again, "What on earth have you
Got to do with it, what's that to you? Come on, just
Say your own confession and succumb." I answered,
"I await the worthier one." but heard this plainly,
"There are yet no blessings for you whatsoever."
"Standing at the foothills of my mountain
I dwell and no one yet has dared to tell me
What you've told me." I answered, softly crying,
"And although I talked to people, still my speeches
Just drifted by and caught no one's attention."

«Заратустра, тот кто горы может двигать,
Сможет двинуть и долины и низины.
Знай, ведь самые тишайшие слова
Производят, управляя миром, бурю.
Ты пойдёшь как тень, предшествуя судьбине:
Управляют миром мысли, что ступают
Голубиными шагами еле слышно».
Я ответил: «Не могу, стесняюсь». — Хохот
Был ответом, разрывавшим сердце болью:
«Ты ещё ребёнком станешь без стесненья,
Гордость юности тебе пока мешает.
Ты незрелым для своих плодов предстанешь,
Если юность не поборешь ты ребёнком».

***

Охмуряет небо осень,
Выпекая, как в печи,
Средь угрюмой чащи сосен
Из туманов калачи.
Завлекает вечер чащу,
Заволакивая сном.
Льёт сапфировая чаша
Свет рубиновым вином.
Натянула туча-сватья —
Сны заката горячи —
На рубиновое платье
Плащ агатовый ночи.

"Zarathustra, he who is able to move great mountains
Can just as well move low-lying lands and valleys.
You should know, after all, the quietest words
Governing the world can bring on stormy tempests.
You shall precede your fate just like a shadow:
It is thoughts that tread with doves' footsteps in silence,
With barely a sound, which guide the world in secret."
I replied, "I can't and I'm ashamed." His laughter
Answered, tearing my heart with pain excruciating,
"You shall yet become a child without such shyness,
For now the pride of youth retards your progress.
You'll appear unripe before your fruitful offspring
If you don't surmount your youth, becoming childlike."

***

Autumn overcasts the heavens
Baking as if in a stove
Crescent rolls of foggy leaven
Midst the murky pine-tree grove.
Evening lures the thicket, glowing
With a dream-enshrouding shine;
Heaven's sapphire cup o'erflowing
With deep light, like ruby wine.
Cloud has made her match beloved —
Sunset's dreams are hot and bright —
She her ruby dress has covered
With the coat of agate night.

www.ingramcontent.com/pod-product-compliance
Lightning Source LLC
Chambersburg PA
CBHW060755050426
42449CB00008B/1419